J. E. Richards,
Boston Theo. Sem.
Dec. 3, 1870

DISCOURSES

ON

THE LORD'S PRAYER.

BY E. H. CHAPIN.

BOSTON:
N. E. UNIVERSALIST PUBLISHING HOUES,
No. 37 Cornhill.
1866.

TO

THE SOCIETY AND CONGREGATION

BEFORE WHOM

THESE DISCOURSES WERE DELIVERED,

THIS BOOK

IS AFFECTIONATELY INSCRIBED

BY

THE AUTHOR.

CONTENTS.

DISCOURSE I.

DISCOURSE II.

DISCOURSE III.

DISCOURSE IV.

DISCOURSE V.

DISCOURSE VI.

DISCOURSE VII.

DISCOURSE VIII.

DISCOURSE IX.

PREFACE.

The plan and purpose of this series are stated in the preliminary remarks in the first discourse. It has not been my object to give a critical exposition of the Lord's Prayer, but to draw from it those practical suggestions which may at once enable us to repeat it with a more intelligent and devout spirit, and to act out the great truths which it involves in our daily work and conversation. In short, the great result which I aim at in these discourses is that state of heart and conduct in which we shall utter this prayer both with our lips and with our lives. The reader of this book, then, need not expect to find in it anything new in thought or interpretation, but I trust that whoever may take it up for the purpose of quickening his religious affections, and animating him in the Christian life, may not be disappointed—may find some help and profit.

I am conscious, however, that but little is said here compared with what might be, upon this pregnant and beautiful formula. Like all our Savior's teachings, we detect in it new suggestions each time that we examine it—we find in it truths that cannot be exhausted, and meanings that cannot be expressed. But my labors such as they are, and with the object which I have stated, are here presented. May they be blessed of Him to whom so may ages and conditions of humanity have lifted and will lift this prayer, and may they contribute something to the advancement of his cause who taught us to utter it.

E. H. C.

New-York, Dec. 11th, 1849.

DISCOURSES

ON THE

LORD'S PRAYER.

DISCOURSE I.

"Our Father which art in heaven."—Matthew vi: 9.

I INVITE your attention for a few Sabbath evenings, to a series of discourses upon the Lord's Prayer. It is not my purpose to enter into any critical disquisition upon this great Formula. Some of its general characteristics, and some reflections pertaining to it as a whole, I reserve for my concluding remarks. But I propose to make each sentence the text of a sermon, and to draw from the truth it affirms, or suggests, its practical applications to the workings of Christianity and the condition of the world, to human life, and to the individual heart. At the same time it will be my endeavor to excite that sentiment of devotion which this Prayer is intended to assist, and to explain its several passages. Thus, in fact, I shall aim to induce the end of all real prayer, which consists both of action and aspiration, of inward communion and of outward conduct—which is, essentially, a desire, a worship, and a work. The clearer our apprehension of truth—the more intense and personal our experience of it—the richer and the deeper will be our devotion. While, on the other hand, the more fervent and habitual our devotion, the quicker shall we detect, the more shall we know, the better shall we obey, the truth. The man who merely *says* the Lord's Prayer, as a prescribed routine of words, evidently does not feel the sentiments which it breathes, nor see the great doctrines which it affirms. I shall consider it in these discourses, then, both as a *Series of Truths*, and a *Form of Devotion*, and if thus, to any degree, I may be instrumental in producing the two-fold result which has been spoken of, I shall indeed be glad, and upon that endeavor I now humbly invoke the Blessing of God.

The Lord's Prayer appropriately commences with the words of the text. God, who is the object of all true worship, is the primary Idea of all being. His existence alone explains the existence of anything. Atheism is not only irreligious, it is absurd. It not only denies the great postulate of faith and of devotion, but it breaks the whole chain of physical causation and of material necessity. For there must be a Cause, else whence all these effects? There must be an independent Power, else upon what do all these things rely?—that Power must be intelligent, else whence come this mutual correspondence, this order, and this harmony? Therefore, if the universe is a mere machine, if matter is the only reality, still its beginning and its end must be God.

But matter is not the only reality. There is a class of facts which a mere intellectual Force, or pantheistic Essence, does not satisfy. The *moral* nature of man—the region of conscience and the will—requires something more than the abstract Deity of the philosopher. The existence of the will, indicates the existence of a Sovereignty which the will should obey. The motions of conscience demonstrate a Law of which conscience is the suggestion. The God of the physical universe is also a *moral* Being, else our moral nature is inexplicable. He is the Source of virtue and the Sanction of duty.

But God is the source of virtue, and the sanction ot duty, because He is the *best* Being. Duty is binding, and virtue supreme, because these meet and mingle in the character of *Infinite Goodness.* God, considered only as a King and a Lawgiver, does not fill the whole sphere of being. There is still a class of facts not accounted for by the existence of One who only ordains conscience and commands the will, any more than these moral faculties are accounted for by a mere Intellectual Force that constructs the flower and moves the planet. In our nature there are quenchless *affections,* yearning sympathies and eager desires. These call for something more than God the Creator, or God the Ruler. Stirred by these, we ask the all-important question—"*What* is this Infinite Being by whose fiat we exist, and whose law we are commanded to obey? What is His disposition toward us? What are our relations to Him?" We cannot escape His presence—we are nothing before His power. He wraps us about more intimately than the light, or the air. He holds us in the hollow of His hand. One motion of his will, and we appear—flakes of being drifting across the abyss of eternity! One breath of His nostrils, and we pass away! How *inevitable* is our condition! We cannot alter its great circumstances. The irresistible current of existence bears us along. We cannot deny life, nor hinder death. We cannot climb beyond the bars of our earthly dwelling-place, nor change our own essential nature. And what a wonderful and awful thought is the bare idea of *being!* How startling, when we stop and seriously think of it! And what a strange existence is this in which we are involved,—made up of permanence and mutation, crossed with good and evil. And here we are, thus ordained, thus controlled, surrounded by these lights and shadows, swinging among these glittering islands and these gulfs of mystery! And, I repeat, *all* is not satisfied when we learn that these skillful forms about us had a Maker, and that these sanctions within us have a Source. The affections, the clinging sympathies, the mounting desires of every man, cry out—"*What* is God? How does He regard me? What are the ties between us? What are His purposes concerning me?" These sentiments find rest, and these questions are answered, when we ascertain that God is *ood*; that goodness is His essential nature; that this is the soul of all His attributes, and the spring of all His purposes; that this prompted His creative work, and dictates His moral rule—and thus, in *this* expression of God, the whole circle of being is accounted for, and satisfied.

And yet, in order that we may consistently apprehend this truth, in order that it may have a fixed and clear expression for us, something more is needed than a *mental conception* of God. Though reason may find out His nature, and the soul acknowledge it, we cannot thus grasp the idea of Infinity, or intensely realize His relation to us. Though His character flashes out in every sunbeam and His presence is felt in every breath of wind, yet, while having no clue but *nature*, man forms confused and partial notions of Him, sinking into the grossness of idolatry, or soaring among the mazes of philosophy; making God a mighty abstraction, or a deformed embodiment; with a beautiful Pantheism, conceiving Him as the universal and inseparable essence of nature, or, with a hideous devotion, carving His image in wood and stone.

We need an *objective representation*, a *personal expression* of God. We need some name that shall signify the complete qualities of His Nature—that shall combine our sublimest, devoutest, and tenderest ideas of Him. We want an image of the Deity that this finite intellect can steadily see, that this wandering will and insufficient conscience can intelligently represent and obey, that this yearning and agitated heart can rest upon and love; and we want one epithet which shall express all these characteristics at the same time—which shall tell their essential unity and speak their highest meaning. My friends, that Image has been given us in Jesus Christ. That epithet he has taught us in that word expressive at once of the giving of life, the claims of authority, and the quality of goodness—that name of cause, and veneration, and love —the name of *Father*.

This, then, is why I said that the Lord's Prayer appropriately begins as it does, not only with God, who is the object of all devotion, but with a name significant of His full nature, of His peculiar relations to us. Not only with a name which even the old Pagan might use, but with a name which Christ alone has taught us, and which he alone has illustrated. And this great truth—the Paternity of God—which he has bid us remember in the solemn act of prayer, is, as it seems to me, the vital truth of the Gospel. I need not tell you that the term in the text is not a solitary one. It was frequent on the lips of Christ. He came especially to exhibit the great fact which it affirms. Nor can I believe that it is used in any sense which forbids its universal application. All may employ it. It expresses God's relation to all. Whatever may be the limitation of the term under peculiar circumstances, its essential interpretation is exhibited in the very spirit of Christianity; its broad scope, its mighty meaning, is illustrated in the parable of the Prodigal Son.

But let us consider more specifically this truth of God's Paternity, and thus, while we detect its essential significance, we shall find further evidence of its application to all men In what sense, then, is God our Father? We have often used this epithet;—do we really understand it? It may be a cardinal article of our faith, but is it only a trite and unconsidered proposition with us? Is it the sincere expression of our moral nature, the conviction of our reason and the testimony of our experience? God is not our Father simply, as the Author of our existence. If so, then is He Father to the clod of the valley, and the drop of dew. But this title expresses a quality different from mere creative energy. It declares a relation which the Deity does not sustain to all things. Not in the sense in which He is the former of our bodies is he the Father of our spirits. Nor, again, is God our Father simply as our Benefactor. For then He would be Father to the beast of the field and the bird of the air. But something more is implied in the relationship we are now considering than mere Goodness —the Benevolence that appears in the adaptations and provides for the wants of every sentient being. Nor should we conceive the Paternity of God as the overflow of an indiscriminate Good-will. We should not dishonor it, by attributing to it any weakness or incongruity. It is perfectly compatible with justice and sovereignty, with chastisement and discipline, with pain and sorrow.

God is our Father in a *spiritual* sense. He is our Father, because we alone, of all earthly existences, bear His image. Because, in finite degree, we have a nature like His own. As man was the crowning act of His creation, so was he distinguished from the rest of His works. Those He called into being by a word; this He molded with peculiar care, and into it He breathed a *living soul.* He evinces His Paternal relation to us, not merely through the general bounties of nature, but by the special gifts of Revelation—not alone by the benignant privilege, but by the solicitous discipline of life. Not only does He bestow upon us animal comforts, but He seeks to impart to us more of His own character. In one word, like the good earthly parent, He *educates* us. And this education is to be attained not by easy indulgence and perpetual enjoyment, but by unstinted exertion, through conflicts, trials, bitter experiences. All that tends to make us spiritually pure, strong and free, exhibits more clearly the relation between God and man and shows that it is a peculiar relation.

It is obvious, then, that the Paternity of God is not limited to any class of men, because every man has the spiritual peculiarities to which that relation is attached. The most feeble and degraded of our race is separated by a broad line from all other creatures. There is a moral deep in him, a spiritual power, which, obscured as it is, is not the possession of any other earthly being, and is a dim image of the eternal. Under the cloud of sin and the corruptions of sensualism, there is embosomed an essence which reflects the overshadowing of its Infinite Original, and sparkles in response to the uncreated Light. His are unlimited capacities and an independent will. His are ceaseless aspirations, and immortal longings. His is a divine birth-right, depraved but not wholly obliterated—a nature not intrinsically mean, but alienated and discrowned. Yes, of the most ignorant savage, of the vilest wretch we spurn, we may say all this. He is a child of the Infinite Spirit. God is his Father. His Father, not in any abstract and metaphorical sense, but in a relation whose scope and intensity, whose grandeur and tenderness, overwhelm our thoughts and far exceed our expression.

And yet, while God is thus essentially the Father of *all* men, there is a practical sense in which He is specially the Father of *some.* He was the Father of Christ in a respect in which He is not our Father, and He is the Father of the good, in a sense in which He is not the Father of the bad. This may be termed not so much a change in Him, as a peculiarity of condition in us. Just in proportion as we realize our spiritual nature, we realize our relation to Him. We perceive Him to be our Father in the degree in which we perceive the grounds of that Paternity. Essentially, I repeat, He is the Father of all men; but practically, subjectively, He is not the Father of the man who forgets His existence, overlooks His Providence, disregards His requirements, and in fact, lives "without God in the world." For there are no filial aspirations in the heart of such a man. He has no child-like trust, or communion. To him, there is no spiritual life in the motions of the universe, no expression of infinite tenderness upon its face. Worshipping the objects of sense, he does not notice the intense longings of his own soul. Swept in the sounding tide of passion, he hears not "the still, small voice," inviting to a holier and serener course. God's love is over him, and God's mercy waits on him; but, in his sensualism and sin, he does not see the Father. He does not realize his relationship to God, and, therefore, so far as it depends upon his action, that relationship is as though it were not.

Here, too, is the man of mere *intellect*, who sees only with the acute but narrow vision of logic; whose head has no arterial connection with his heart; whose dry light of reason retains no glow from the affections. He sees nothing in the transfigured aspect of beauty, or through the atmosphere of love. To him, the unrolled ocean suggests only depth and quantity, and the heavens sparkle merely with mathematical diagrams. He constructs nicely-balanced theories, but they are as cold as they are clear, and untrue because they are partial. He sees only with the intellect. He rests upon no basis profounder than the intellect. He lacks sympathy, he lacks moral enthusiasm, he lacks religious life. Having no affectionate affinities, he does not feel or see the Paternity of God. To him, the Deity is merely a First Cause, an abstract Intelligence.

But, to the man of spiritual aims and devout sentiment, of pure affections and of right reason, there is no truth so great, so central, so apparent, as this of the Paternity of God. The Gospel is full of it. It appears in every lineament of the universe. It is the meaning of creation, the explanation of human history, the horizon of reconciliation that broods around all the mystery of life. The man who believes this great truth, always holds in his bosom a conscious joy and an everlasting spring of hope. He is never alone. Nothing to him appears empty, or desolate. The solitary chamber, the savage desert, for him is filled with a Being whom he loves and adores. He throws open his window to the night-sky, and, while all is still and slumbering below, above him, farther than eye can reach or thought ascend kindles the outspread glory of the Father. He rejoices to come with filial trust in all perplexities, and shelter himself under this brooding Paternity. He feels the heart of infinite Love beating close to his heart, and throbbing through all the pulses of the universe. Nor is this the emotion of diluted sentiment. God's essential Paternity lends glory to all His attributes; His Wisdom, Justice, Truth and Power—it kindles in the soul a loftier and serener spirit of devotion, touches the spring of penitence, and makes us good because He is good. Evil men may proclaim the Fatherhood of God with their lips. But it is not the bad and the weak, who really comprehend its meaning. The deeper our moral life and the keener our spiritual vision, the clearer appears this truth. The more we are like Christ, the more do we realize it, the more confidingly do we rest under it, the closer does it make our communion, with more profound significance do we say—"Our Father which art in heaven!"

Such is the sense in which God is our Father, and the Father of all men. He is our Father and theirs, because we are all spiritual beings. And, yet, this relation, comparatively, is as though it were not, until we realize it. We realize it as we become more and more like Him. In bringing these remarks to a close, then, let me urge upon you the importance of realizing this truth, that you may understand the words with which you commence this prayer, that you may strive for that spiritual condition in which only you can truly know Him whom you address.

First, then, it is important we should realize that God is our Father, in order that we may have right views of *Religion.* How essential such views are to our conduct and our peace, I need not say. We do not all live as we believe—we do not carry out practically the utmost inferences of our creed. Some of us are worse, it may be some of us are better than our faith. But yet in some degree our faith affects our character—to a great extent, it colors our view of life. If God is the beginning of all things, He is, in a peculiar sense, the beginning of our religion. Our highest endeavors after virtue will be attempts to imitate Him. Our decision upon specific questions of right and wrong will be governed by our conceptions of the Divine nature. We shall religiously cherish those sentiments of which He is the absolute Expression. The view which we entertain of Him, affects the whole spirit of the New-Testament. This is the radical interpretation of texts and doctrines. Should God appear as a different Being from what He does now, the whole burden of the Gospel would be changed to us. On the other hand, he who has been wandering in the maze of false conceptions, and upon whom, at length, has burst the truth of God's Paternity, opens his Bible as a new book. Christianity spreads around him a firmament of sudden glory, and reveals to his eye unexpected riches.

Again, it is important we should realize the truth of God's Paternity, because of its *consolations*. I have just said that it reconciles the mysteries of life. To the purpose of the great Father we must often refer these mysteries. "That God has some good end in view," is the conviction that enables us to bear up under them. Our reason cannot penetrate them. All evil, in fact the very existence of evil, is inexplicable until we refer to the Paternity of God. It hangs a huge blot in the universe, until the orb of Divine Love rises behind it. In that apposition we detect its meaning. It appears to us but a finite shadow as it passes across the disc of Infinite light. It is not necessary for me to specify the instances in which the truth of "God our Father," brings strength and peace to the human soul. How deeply is it illustrated in the experience of many a heart beating around me! Without any God, how awful would be the course of life! We should be drifting across the sea of time, without an end and without a meaning. Again, without the knowledge of God's character, our journey though guided would still be overshadowed with changeful uncertainties. But now, knowing that He is our Father, through the storm and the night we may trustingly proceed, for the star of His compassion never sets, and He spans our voyage with a zodiac of promises.

Once more; this great truth furnishes us with the profoundest motives to *obedience.* The basis of all genuine service is *love.* He who demands the surrender of our will, and the devotion of our hearts, beams upon us with all the claims of his character. How can we turn from such a service? What bliss in that loyal acquiescence, in that conscious communion! What agony, what loss, in that alienation and neglect! What motive to repentance stronger than God's Paternity? What encouragement to rise from our sins, more inspiring than His grace? What sanction mightier to bind us to His law, than the Love that was manifested for us in the bleeding sacrifice of the cross? What sting of retribution keener than the thought of His abused mercies and His slighted proffers? Oh! the doctrine of God's Paternity, in its full glory, in its solemn sweetness, is anything but a weakening influence in the soul—is anything but an incitement to sin. If we would only *realize* it, we should burst these fetters of self-will; we should leap from this apathy and indulgence; with unsealed hearts, with a keen and joyful shame, we should cry—"Our Father which art in heaven!"

Thus have I endeavored to lead you to some considerations suggested by the Text. In this light, then, consider the first sentence of the Lord's Prayer. "In this manner," says the Savior, "therefore pray ye." As though assuredly we *would* pray. As though we would do that which he taught both by precept and example. As though we might be perplexed about the method, but did not lack in disposition. And, yet, how many do lack in the disposition! How many slight this high privilege of devotion; rush from their chambers in the morning, drop into the silence of slumber at night, mingle with the temptations, and sins, and cares of the world, without a single uplifting of the heart to God, without once seeking communion with Him whom angels worship, and who graciously waits to hear! Yes, in this course of weakness and uncertainty, of human need below and Divine help above, there are those who never pray—or with whom prayer is the last resort in calamity and dismay.

Yet we should pray, and prayer should be with us an habitual reality of the soul, a supreme delight in the happiest hours of life, as well as a resource in its troubled seasons. And when we pray, let us say, "Our Father which art in heaven." "*Our* Father." The Father of all men. The Religion of Christ is individual in its requirements, but general in its applications. It demands the solitary discipline and the social work, and even in our most secret devotions we must not indulge the limitations of selfishness, but remember all with whom God has linked us, and for whom we should labor; remember all, kindred, friends, enemies, the world.

"Which *art*," now even as of old, then manifest on the mountain and in the thunder, but now breathing into our souls the suggestions of His spirit, and the strength of His help. "Which art in *heaven*." In the region of spiritual life, everywhere where the heart will seek and the thought ascend.

With these conceptions, let us come and say—"Our FATHER!" Yes, thus is the majesty of God brought down to us. Thus is His Infinity personified. Thus is His exhaustless Love tenderly expressed. Without this, how awful, how overwhelming, would be the act of devotion! Science is daily revealing to us a wider scope and a loftier grandeur in the universe. To the exploring eye it opens new vistas of creation, and pours upon its dazzled vision the brightness of innumerable suns. And, among these, dimly swings this atom of a world, and far beyond all reaches the Infinity of God! How could we have confidence to look up to Him, through all these countless myriads and this intolerable splendor? And, again, when we consider His Holiness and our impurity, the awfulness of God and the insignificance of man, were it not for His own help, we should not dare to approach Him. But this revelation of "The FATHER" has swept away all the barriers of distance, it has streamed into our souls through all the glories of the universe, it has touched us with the intimate nearness, the infinite condescension of God, and gathered into that one name all that is venerable with all that is lovely. Let us habitually avail ourselves, then, of the privilege made known to us. In every experience of life, let us bring to His footstool hearts of reverence and of penitence, of holy desire and of filial trust.

DISCOURSE II.

"Hallowed be thy name."—Matthew vi: 9.

In the preceding discourse we considered the meaning of the term "Father," as applied to God. Standing at the commencement of this formula, that term fixes our minds upon the nature of Him whom we approach. It defines the great object of our supplication and our worship. The sentence—"Our Father which art in heaven," being, therefore, a form of address, the text constitutes the first desire, or petition, of the Lord's Prayer.

The connection between this and the preceding clause, however, is not accidental but essential. In the natural order of things, we cannot pray "Hallowed be thy name," until we know what that name is; and, when we do know it, we cannot refrain from this as the next and immediate expression. It is the outbursting flame of a kindled heart. It is the spontaneous utterance of a soul rapt with the excellence of God, and postponing its personal requests in a general desire.

I have said that these words constitute the first petition

in the Lord's Prayer. But, in fact, they are not wholly a petition. The sentiment which breathes through them, combines both petition and adoration. It mingles the incense of homage with the earnestness of a wish. It is what we say to God alone, of ourselves, upon the revelation of His Fatherhood, and with our thoughts fixed in contemplation of His attributes. It is a lyrical exclamation, an irrepressible hallelujah. And yet, I repeat, it is a prayer also. We *ask* as well as say—"Hallowed be thy name." The very fact that we sincerely adore that Name, implies a desire in our hearts that others also may render homage to it, and that we ourselves may honor it better. As a *prayer* then, breaking out from the centre of a devout worship, as a prayer that ourselves and others may be more devout, I propose chiefly to consider it in this discourse.

The form of expression in the text may be treated in two ways. We may thus pray that God would hallow His own Name, or that we, His children, may hallow it. This two-fold petition, then, will separate my remarks under two heads.

I. In breathing this prayer, we ask that *God would hallow His own Name, or cause it to be hallowed.* The amount of this petition, the condition of its fulfillment, is, simply, this—that our Father in heaven would make Himself known, would more and more reveal Himself unto us and unto all men. This clear knowledge is the only contingent in the case; certainly it is an essential contingent. Surely, a full and steady perception of God, would melt every heart in homage before Him. For what is it to hallow God's name? It is to reverence it. And what is reverence? Upon what does it depend? To what does it attach itself? I answer, in the first place, that it is not the tribute which we pay to mere power and magnitude, even though these should dilate to infinity. We *cannot* reverence these unmingled with other qualities. *Nature* appears to us in forms of greatness, and with manifestations of power. We are thrilled with admiration, we crouch in awe, before its revelations. We are lifted up with emotions of sublimity. But we do not *reverence* any of these. We never apply this term in regard to the material universe, filled as it is with irresistible forces, and immeasurable magnitudes. Neither do we reverence mere power, when exhibited by man. We may be astonished or terrified at the dominion of a monarch, or the triumphs of a warrior. But we do not reverence the mere greatness that is symbolized by a throne, or the success that is crowned with reeking laurels. Nor can we reverence even a great intellect, separated from every other quality. True, intellectual energy is immensely superior to the physical force of nature, or the circumstantial power of the king and the hero. Far better than the tribute that we render in palaces, or pay to victorious soldiers, is the sentiment with which we honor that master-power beneath which all material laws are plastic, which searches the secrets of the universe, and binds us in its chain of demonstration. But call this sentiment wonder, admiration, enthusiasm, what we will, it is not that peculiar, that mingled feeling which we term reverence. This sentiment, I repeat, is not rendered to mere power, or greatness, nay not even to moral power—where the qualities displayed are merely persistence and energy.

But, on the other hand, neither do we reverence mere *kindness, amiability, affection.* These qualities win our esteem and our love. They may even glorify a character that is deficient in other respects. They may compensate for many deformities. They may, at times, impart their innate energy to dullness, indolence, and timidity. But, after all, they are not sufficient to stir up that profound and peculiar feeling which we are now considering. Sometimes degenerating into weakness, and absolute vice, even in their best estate they lack that intrinsic dignity which always abides in the object we truly reverence.

Reverence, my friends, is a sentiment of combined awe and love, of filial trust and obedient homage. There are few to whom it can be rendered, and these must blend in their nature both power and tenderness, greatness and sympathy, authority and affection. In one word, they must be *good,* not in the sentimental and hackneyed, but in the simplest and high-toned sense. None can so justly claim it on earth as they who really fulfil the parental relation, and, therefore, in ascribing the name of Father to the Infinite One, we also ascribe to Him those qualities that demand our reverence magnified to infinite extent. God is to be reverenced, for in Him Power and Love, Authority and Condescension, mingle in perfect harmony. And just in proportion as His nature breaks out upon us in all its fullness, we shall perceive its demands upon us, and it will be hallowed.

Now the importance of a full knowledge of God, in order that He may be truly reverenced, truly worshiped and hallowed, is seen in the existence of two great errors, each resting upon a religious basis. The first of these, is *superstition.* They who are misled by its influence, are, perhaps, more than any, so far as mere professions go, strenuous for the worship of God, and the sanctions of religion. In fact, it generally passes under the name of religion, and it is animated by a solicitous reference to the Deity. In one form or another, God is besought, God is invoked. Temples are decorated to His honor, and altars steam with His worship. The Druid smears his robes with human blood, and the Fakir cuts himself with knives. In all this there is worship—but it is an awful worship. There is a deep sense of God—but He is a God pavilioned in thunder, and clothed with dreadful flame. The Deity is seen as Greatness and Power, but His Love and His Mercy are obscured. Or, if the light of Revelation has modified these savage conceptions, and dispelled these gross externals, in how many instances do men act not from the sentiment of reverence but from that of terror, and worship God, essentially, as only infinite Greatness, or absolute Power! To such, Religion is not a fresh reality, but a tradition and a form. Duty is not the absolute Right, but an arbitrary routine. Faith is not rational, but imperative. They speak of "the love of God," and of its inward experience, yet how often is this a strained and wavering emotion, sometimes overflowing in a bigoted zeal, sometimes wrapped in a feverish mysticism. It is not a spontaneous emotion. Its interior spring is terror, and its expression is constrained and fearful. The joy of *true* love is not in it. It does not spring up, like living water, everlastingly. About this kind of religion—if we should term it religion—there is a cloistered narrowness and unreality. The ample air and the glad light are not in it. God's benignity does not overarch the universe. His benevolence does not animate the lineaments of nature. His loving-kindness does not consecrate the mysteries of life.

His Presence is not a consoling and uplifting idea in the soul. He is the Deity of the Law, not of the Gospel—the Sovereign who spoke through the thick cloud and he trumpet-blast, not the Father who beamed in Jesus Christ. He is to be served only in one circle of duty, in one sphere of action, not in various forms of conduct. He is found only in vaulted churches, or in a "dim, religious light," of retirement; not in the scenery of nature and on the face of the outward world, in the pomp of the heavens and the festival of the flowers, in the realities of history and the open communions of daily life. Now this idea of religion, this idea of God, whatever its symbols or its name, is superstitious. It is partial. It conceives only a Deity of absolute Power and infinite Authority. Its *terror* is not *reverence.* God is *worshiped.* but His name is not truly *hallowed.*

The other religious error to which I referred, as indicating a partial knowledge of God, and in which, therefore, His name is not truly hallowed, may be called an *Epicurean laxity,* or *un*-moral sentimentalism. In this view, the Deity is virtually regarded as merely a *good-natured* Being, too gracious to punish sin, and too tender to inflict pain. According to this system, evil itself is very often defined as an unsubstantial negation, the reverse side of goodness, and sin as a necessity, or misfortune on the part of man. The benevolence of God, as it appears in the department of natural theology, is much dwelt upon. In the volume of Revealed Religion, the *promises* of the Gospel almost exclusively occupy the attention. Now, out of this arise many amiable and noble conceptions. The heart is frequently warmed with generous incentives, and swept by gushes of devout rapture. The universe throbs with perpetual gladness, and life is lighted up with everlasting hope. But, after all, this theory is defective. It is exclusive and superficial. It lacks moral depth and stringency. The great sanctions of duty, the dignity and responsibility of free-agency, the profoundest definitions and the highest ends of goodness, the excellence and necessity of holiness, do not appear in it—or appear but faintly. It does not contain that which prostrates a man with humility, and smites him with contrition; which sends him in to search his own heart, and to wrestle earnestly with his own nature, his passions, and motives, and principles of life. The *guilt* of sin is not sufficiently felt and pondered. It presents too few incentives to prayer, to deep, personal meditation. Virtue is regarded rather as mere innocence than an athletic attainment, demanding all the powers, and comprehending the highest results of the soul. It induces no course of spiritual discipline, of inner life and growth. Nor is this to be explained merely by saying, that those who occupy this position have adopted religion as a set of opinions and a code of moralities, rather than a principle of personal and spiritual life—as a *view* of truth, rather than an *experimental application* of it. This is true ; but it is also true that the error has sprung from a partial conception of God. He has been considered as a kind and merciful Being, but not sufficiently in His moral nature and His majesty. And this partial conception exists, perhaps, because men have not entered enough into their own moral natures, but have looked too much upon the surface of things. Yet, whatever may be the original processes of this error, I repeat it subsists upon a partial conception of God. He is not only a tender Benefactor, but a moral Ruler, to whom virtue, rectitude, holiness, is supreme. He is the *best* Being. He is truly "the Father of our spirits," because in Him justice blends with mercy, righteousness with kindness, purity with condescension, and His benignity is one with infinite power and infinite authority. He is supremely good, but goodness, my friends, is not indiscriminating affection—is not a sentiment which would dictate the bestowal of immediate ease regardless of ends—but, for the sake of permanent, righteous and blessed ends, it often prevents immediate ease. And in nothing is the goodness of God more evident than in the fact that He has precipitated man upon the balance of *free-agency,* that by his own choice and by the efforts of his own will, he might attain not only the bliss but the intrinsic life and power of virtue. In nothing is the goodness of God more evident than in the fact that, as man *is* a free-agent, he has been made subject to moral sanctions, and placed in a world of discipline, for only by spiritual struggles within, and impediments of evil without, could he attain the end and the glory of free-agency. This system, therefore, which insists only upon the exterior benevolence of God, and holds this only as a perception, or as the agent of fitful emotion, and which takes but feebly into the account—if at all—His righteousness, His justice, His inward requirements, I term *un*-moral, and merely sentimental; and affirm that it does not represent the fullness, it does not completely define the goodness of God. It does not over-rate the Love of God—its power, extent, endurance; God himself *is* Love;—but it does not fully show how that Love manifests itself, what is its end, and what is its process. By this theory, God's name is *acknowledged* but not *hallowed*—He is worshiped in *gladness* but not in *reverence.*

Thus, when we pray—"Hallowed be thy name," we may ask that God would manifest himself more fully For we see that the gravest errors issue from undue conceptions of Him; error itself is the partial perception rather than the total ignorance of truth. In breathing this petition, we desire that God would reveal Himself as He *is*, and thus dispel our false images of Him. For too much we fashion God after our own hearts, and project an idea of Him from among the lights and shadows of our own souls. In saying—"Hallowed be thy name," we pray that God would beam out in the blended qualities of His nature. So, everywhere, shall the altars of superstition crumble, its fearful rites cease, its mental clouds disperse in that great light. So, everywhere, shall a superficial morality and a nerveless sentimentalism, be changed to a strenuous virtue and a devout life.

II. But I pass to the second division of my discourse, and remark that, with these same words, we can also pray that *we*, that *all men;* may hallow the name of God. Nay, my friends, virtually, we *do* make this petition, or else we use the words in mockery. We do not really desire that God's name may be hallowed, unless we resolve ourselves to reverence it. That is no prayer which does not join conduct to aspiration. We say—"Our Father which art in heaven, hallowed be thy name," but the pointed question presses home upon us—do *we* hallow it?—do we *mean* to hallow it? Or does it signify nothing with us? Is it merely a form that we learned in childhood? A familiar petition, that we mutter without regard to what it implies or requires? If, on the other hand, this is a sincere prayer with us, then will we resolve and endeavor to consecrate this great Name on our *lips,* in our *lives,* and in our *hearts.* To these three points I propose to devote the concluding portion of my discourse.

First, then, if we would use this prayer sincerely, we must hallow God's name upon our *lips.* It will never be a light word there. It will never drop out in jest, or ring in blasphemy. I wish to touch this point earnestly. I would speak strongly against the common sin of *Profaneness.* Are there any before me who are accustomed to use God's name as an expletive, and to bandy it as a by-word? Who employ it in all kinds of conversation, and throw it about in every place? Perhaps, in their hearts, they consider this habit as an *accomplishment!* think it manly and brave to *swear!* Let me say, then, that profaneness is a *brutal* vice. He who indulges it is no gentleman. I care not what his stamp may be in society. I care not what clothes he wears, or what culture he boasts. Despite all his refinement, the light and habitual taking of God's name, betrays a coarse nature, and a brutal will. Nay, he tacitly admits that it is ungentlemanly. He restrains his oaths in the presence of ladies; and he who fears not to rush into the chancery of heaven and swear by the Majesty there, is decently observant in the drawing-room and the parlor. But, again, Profaneness is an *unmanly* and *silly* vice. It certainly is not a grace in conversation, and it adds no strength to it. There is no organic symmetry in the narrative that is ingrained with oaths; and the blasphemy that bolsters an opinion does not make it any more correct. Our mother-English has variety enough to make a story sparkle, and to give point to wit; it has toughness and vehemence enough to furnish the sinews for a debate and to drive home a conviction; without degrading the holy epithets of Jehovah. Nay, the use of these expletives, argues a limited range of ideas, and a consciousness of being on the wrong side. And if we can find no other phrases through which to vent our choking passion, we had better repress that passion. And, again, Profaneness is a *mean* vice. It indicates the grossest ingratitude. According to general estimation, he who repays kindness with contumely, he who abuses his friend and benefactor, is deemed pitiful and wretched. And yet, oh profane man! whose name is it you handle so lightly? It is that of your best Benefactor! You, whose blood would boil to hear the venerable names of your earthly parents hurled about in scoffs and jests, abuse, without compunction and without thought, the name of your heavenly Father! Finally, Profaneness is an *awful* vice. Once more I ask, Whose name is it you so lightly use? That name of God!—have you ever pondered its meaning? Have you ever thought *what* it is that you mingle thus with your passion and your wit? It is the name of

Him whom the angels worship, and Whom the heaven of heavens cannot contain!

Surely, then, we cannot sincerely breathe the petition of the text, if we do not consecrate God's name upon our lips. That Prayer cannot consistently accompany Profaneness. The one will never escape the doors of the mouth, if we utter the other from the heart. Profane man, though habit be ever so stringent with you, when the word of mockery and of blasphemy is about to leap from your lips, think of the considerations just suggested —think of God—and, instead of that rude oath, cry out in reverent prayer "Hallowed be thy name!"

But, in the *second* place, I would say that, in order to utter this Prayer sincerely, we must hallow God's name in our *lives*—in our habitual conduct. Many a man whose lips are clean from oaths, and who never uses God's name lightly, may live without any reference to His claims. Every man *does* live so who has some object that is, practically, higher than God, and that stands in the place of God. How common is the sin of *Idolatry!* Not the worship of graven images, but a pursuit of aims and an application of means showing that men render supreme homage to something else than the true Deity—that His is not the name they habitually honor and hallow. It is not that they have some great temporal object in view which they seek with strenuous effort, but that to this purpose they warp all moral considerations, and sacrifice all religious claims. Where God, by the voice of conscience, or by the written word, indicates one path, they for the sake of their darling object turn into another. While He claims their affections they surrender them to this temporal end, and He is neglected. This, let it appear in what form it will, is *idolatry*. The man who is bent on the gratification of his appetites, whose eyes turn restlessly in quest of delight and whose pulses bound with continual desire, is an idolator. He worships sensual good—the flower-crowned and voluptuous image of *pleasure*, whose ritual is the tinkling cymbal and the circling wine-cup. The monitions of duty and the voice that calls him to higher aims, are unheeded. His energies and his time are exhausted for this one end. The man whose main object is popular fame and popular power, is prone to idolatry. His standard of action is the whim of the multitude, his principles are plastic to their prejudices. Or if he controls them, and plays with cunning upon their passions, his moral code is always level to policy, and works in the traces of an unsanctified ambition. He may endeavor to cheat conscience, and to call his obliquities by a good name, but evidently, he worships reputation and success more than he worships God. The absorbed wealth-seeker is an idolator. His god is gold. No fasts are too painful, no vigils too late, no pilgrimages too remote to secure its favor. He endures willingly and eagerly torrid heat and polar cold, the festering miasma of one climate and the deadly chill of another, the dangers of the wilderness and the ocean. Would he do as much as this for the highest calls of duty? Would he serve the true God, with as much energy and patience? These illustrations, which might be greatly multiplied, are sufficient to show us the necessity of hallowing God's name in daily life, in every pursuit and in every aim.

Finally; we must hallow God's name in our *hearts*. We must cherish reverent thoughts of Him in the inmost recesses of our souls. We must feel His Presence about us, and within us. We must think and act in the awe of that Presence. It must be the greatest of all Realities to us. Without this there can be no true hallowing of His name. Without this we cannot consecrate it in our lives, or respect it with our lips. Without this we shall possess no spring of moral life, no consistency of moral action, no lofty and sacred aim.

We need at the present day, more than anything else, a sense of God. On the whole, ours is an irreverent age. There is a thirst for innovation, an impatience of authority, a contempt for the old and the past, that leaps far beyond the medium-line of truth, and over-steps the limits of honesty as well as of modesty. In the crash of revolutions and the decisions of criticism, in the zeal for reform and the desire for progress, let us not forget that there are some things always venerable. The sentiment of reverence is one of the noblest in human nature, and the heart that is empty of it, is empty of all that ensures the permanence of any morality. And especially, I say, must the sense of God be alive and constant in our souls. Without it we lose the sanctions and the ends of life. Without it we do not truly live. It is this that is lacking in the hearts of those to whose idolatry I have just alluded. Theirs is not merely misdirected activity, but a partial activity—an activity that leaves the deepest channel of humanity dry. They do not live in a sense of God, and, therefore, spiritually, they do not live at all. Certainly, there are many like these whom the Bible pronounces not alive—not alive to their highest interests, not living their best life. In this way a community wrapped up in secularity and sin, with all its gay variety and all its bustle, regarded by a vision of spiritual discernment, seems dead and desolate. Yes, those diligent forms appear as lifeless as the embalmed nations who people the catacombs of Thebes, and the appeals of religion, the incentives to higher life, the moving Presence of God, is as unfelt amid this waste of worldliness, as the wind that sighs over the unconscious sands of the desert.

The great answer, then, that we require to this petition, is that God's name may be hallowed, that His Presence may be realized, in our hearts. With this consciousness, therefore, let us utter it. With the thought of Him as the Infinite whose scope comprehends the universe, and who dwells in the humblest soul; with the thought of Him as the Good, whose bounties are poured continually around us; with the thought of Him as the Holy, whom seraphs perpetually adore; let us pray "Hallowed be thy name!" Oh God! hallow it. Let us see thee more clearly in our joy and our sorrow, in change and immutability, in all the facts of the inner and the outer universe. And in all our agency, in all the action of the world, in its busy marts and its secret chambers, in its seasons of toil and its seasons of devotion, at every period and in every place, in lip, and life, and heart, grant that *we* may hallow it.

DISCOURSE III.

"Thy Kingdom come."—Matthew vi: 10.

We have seen that the first two sentences of the Lord's Prayer have an organic connection. The same relation exists between the words of the text and the preceding clause. When God's name is everywhere hallowed, His kingdom will have come. He will not be truly worshiped, until every land and every heart shall have rendered Him its allegiance. But while the realization of the desire expressed in the text is necessary to the fulfillment of the foregoing petition, on the other hand, the perception of God's character and of true worship, is essential to that *spiritual fraternity* which is so profound an element, and to that *human brotherhood* which is so prominent a feature in the consummation called "the Kingdom of God." There is no bond of union so vital as a common worship. There is no cause of separation so effectual as different ideas of Religion. This is sufficiently illustrated in the sectarian affinities and antipathies immediately about us. And, in looking through the world, this fact becomes more apparent, as religious differences and resemblances are more or less radical. Therefore, I repeat, in praying for the Reign of Heaven, we comprehend the universal knowledge and universal worship of the Father.

Having thus considered the *relative* nature of this petition, let us now proceed to discuss its *burden* and its *object*. In endeavoring to do this, I shall distribute my remarks under three heads.

I. Let us observe the fact that this consummate blessing is to *come*. However correctly, in some instances, the phrase "Kingdom of God," or "Kingdom of Heaven," may be applied to the setting up of the christian dispensation, or to the blessedness of the immortal world, no doubt the original term should frequently be translated "*Reign*," instead of "Kingdom,"—"Reign of God," "Reign of Heaven." It indicates a principle, rather than a form; a progressive force, and not a fixed dominion. In this sense it is employed in the Lord's Prayer, and, therefore, the text should be rendered—"thy Reign come." But, however we render the term, it certainly signifies a consummation not yet attained. The petition "thy Kingdom come!" is as proper now as it was in the days of Jesus. It pertains to a Result that sweeps immeasurably beyond the limits of the Jewish polity—it reaches into ages far remote from the primitive era of the Gospel.

And, although a perfect realization of the Ideal comprehended in that Kingdom may never be accomplished in this world, even for this world it suggests a better condition than any that has yet been experienced.

A great good *to come,* then—a better era for the individual and for the race—this is the first suggestion of the text. The vision of Christianity is *prospective.* Unlike Paganism, its "golden age" is in the future. Whatever theory we may entertain concerning primeval time, with whatever innocence it may have been peopled, with whatever glory adorned, it is not for us to sigh over its lost loveliness, or to cast back wistful glances upon its glimmering gates. The Gospel requires of us diligent hands, prayerful hearts, and a *forward* look. It urges self-sacrifice, but it holds out a glorious expectancy. Humanity is in neither a state of decay, nor of stagnation. It is moving, and moving for the better. Continents of time and mountains of difficulty may stretch between us and that glad era, but a serene light streams down from heaven upon the destinies of the race, and an auroral promise tints the horizon of the future.

But I refer to this prospective attitude of Christianity, because it thus exhibits two characteristics especially worthy our notice. First, *it is in accordance with the general working of God.* Progress is the law of universal being. Everything that can be considered as a permanent whole, at least, is constantly developing. In the physical world, for instance, isolated forms of matter may have their cycles, passing through periods of decline as well as growth. But the material universe, considered as a whole, appears to be always unfolding higher conditions. The operation of this law is manifest in the history of the earth and in the movements of the stars. The conquests of progress are marked in hoary strata, and commemorated by medallions set in solid rock. The firmament over our heads, suggests an uncompleted purpose ; and that its sparkling worlds are only the blossoms of creation.

I need not say that progress is also the law of the human soul. Whatever may be the limitations of mind in other stages of being, we know that here its essential characteristic, and, indeed, one great proof of its immortality, is an ever-unfolding power, retained amid the decay of the body, and plucked from the withering garniture of age.

With this general law of progress, I repeat, Christianity is in beautiful accordance. It is not a fixed system. An everlasting Principle in itself, it has no unchangeable and universal forms. With infinite depths of truth, and an incessant spring of spiritual life, it cannot be limited to any time, or petrified in any shape. It is fluent and eternal. The reconciling element of the world, it goes forth into every age, and responds to the deepest tone of want in every posture of humanity. In fact, for every new epoch it is a new Revelation. It ever demands a present and cannot be confined to a past interpretation. There is always an original meaning—a meaning adapted to the times—in the Miracles and the Teachings, the Cross and the Sepulchre, the Personality and the Life of Jesus. Not that the Gospel essentially changes, but it adjusts itself to the vision of man, or, rather, man sees it from different points of view; not that a jot of its familiar truth grows stale, but each filament unfolds new relations, and assumes a new expression. Now Christianity is a primitive congregation, and now a magnificent hierarchy; now it is Catholic, and now Protestant; now it shelters its life in a conservative monasticism, now it bursts upon the world in the multiform forces of modern civilization; now, as a lax and wilful individualism prevails, it is crowned with Divine authority; now, as mankind are hindered and crushed by a centralizing despotism, it opens with an intense humanity. In one word, Christianity, although introduced by miracle, has fallen into the ordinary current of Providence. Not by external ruptures, and sudden shocks, but with an inner life, it gradually fills every pore and artery. It is adjusted to the conditions of a progressive race. And yet, this adjustment is not a servile compliance, but a condescending and uplifting sympathy. Mingling thus with the conditions of one age, it induces the better estate of another, and creates those yet deeper wants which it alone can satisfy. It exalts humanity by accompanying it, and, ever creating higher ideals, it always appears in the van as the only help and interpretation. It not only awaits man as a glorious kingdom to come; it goes with him, and *prepares* him for that kingdom. It is not only the object of his best hopes, and his devout desires, but it is his guide through the tangled journey of the present. And, while thus we find that it is not a fixed religion, we also see that it did not break at once upon the world with all its power and blessedness. It reserved its consummation for a happier future, which mankind can attain only by prayer and toil. And, no doubt, although now, and ever since its advent, men have found in it inexpressible riches of truth and love, the more exalted natures and the purer vision of that better time, shall detect in it still deeper meanings, and know that it contains an excellence which we can hardly conceive.

The other characteristic presented by Christianity in this prospective attitude, is indicated in the *wise benevolence* of such a position. By proclaiming a better era, it gives to individuals and to the race, the loftiest inspiration of hope. And how essential this sentiment is, I need not say. It is the life of all enterprise and all improvement. Fix man in one posture, or shift him into a retrograde condition, and every noble faculty would be paralyzed. What is true here of the individual, is true of the race. It is possible that there are some so intensely selfish that human good in general, seems of no importance to them. But every true man is interested in the prospects of the race; in the condition of future generations. Every one, to some degree, looks forward beyond his own earthly period, and *does* something that will not affect himself so much as those who will come after him. We cannot forget our interest in this common earth. Though in a few years, at the farthest, its springing life will be nothing to us, and we can engage in its busy schemes no more, though soon it shall hide us in its bosom and unknown multitudes will trample upon our dust, yet, with affectionate curiosity, we ask what *shall* be upon this planet whose sweet light we have enjoyed so much; with an irrepressible sympathy we mix our thoughts and feelings with those of unborn ages. I cannot think there is any man to whom the certainty of a fixed condition for the human race no better than the present would not be disheartening, even though *he* will soon pass out from it. There is no good heart that would not sink with despair to know that mankind is growing worse, and that the future would be more vile than the present, even though that future were thousands of years ahead. Therefore each generation, though living far from its consummation, rejoices to believe that there is a Kingdom to come—a Kingdom of Holiness, Truth, and Love. And each generation, realizing that it is not contributing to a circuitous, or short-lived result, puts forth a more sacred diligence, and builds up a more solid fabric. The best things that men have done, have been those acts of self-sacrifice and of love, which refer, chiefly, to the future. All that inspires the mission of teachers, and the attempts of reformers, all that has nerved philanthropists to toil and martyrs to die, is the prospect of a good argued from the present, but lighting up the summits of distant ages. And, often, when the vision has been too intensely confined to the present; often, when the atmosphere of sensualism wraps itself around us; when the pit of sin yawns open and exposes all its hideous shapes; when Famine staggers unheeded through fields of plenty, and Virtue is stricken down with contemptuous laughter, when Oppression rears his impudent front, and Corruption runs through the streets, the promise implied in this petition—"Thy Kingdom come," murmuring under all the mass of evil, steadies the wavering trust and nerves the drooping arm.

In the fact that this Kingdom is to come, then, we see an evidence of its Divine authenticity. In its adjustment to the law of progress, in its ministration to the uplifting sentiment of hope, we have an answer to the troubled faith, or the skeptical sneer, which asks—why Christianity did not come at once in its full glory, and why, even yet, it has accomplished so little of its work.

II. Let us, in the next place, consider some of the *indications* of that coming. As we have just considered the *gradual* nature of this coming, we cannot expect to discover a great advancement within any narrow scope of time. Our decision as to the success or defeat of any great cause, will depend very much upon our scale of measurement. If we measure by years, or by generations even, it may appear to have gained nothing; nay, owing to the limitation of our vision, it may seem to retrograde, instead of moving, as it really does, steadily onward, as the stars seem to turn backward when we forget the motion of the earth, and mistake it for a fixed centre. In studying the fact of human progress, as affected by Christianity, then, we must employ a standard equal to the magnitude of the movement. We must not consider merely the access or recess in isolated instances. We must examine the tide-water marks of centuries, and then we shall find that the great deep, as a whole, has been heaved up to a higher level. In thirty, or even a hundred years, Christianity may have accomplished comparatively but little—but see what it has done in eighteen-hundred years! There is no need of detailed illustrations of this truth; but let us refresh our consciousness by referring to two or three general instances.

That the Kingdom of God is coming, I would observe, in the first place, is indicated by the fact that the most civilized communities of the world are in a far better condition now, than the same class of communities were before the advent of Jesus. Whatever seasons of corruption may have intervened, there has never been, since then, any absolute decline in society. The pulse of improvement has beat steadily through the most stagnant periods. The darkest ages were lighted by a higher intelligence, and animated by a profounder morality, than Egypt, or Greece, or Rome, in their best estate. Of course, I do not speak now of the sublime and chosen few, but I contrast the *masses* of one epoch with the *masses* of another. And I would bear upon this, as a main point—that the general operation of Christianity is to be compared with the general operation of elements which existed before it, and that its progressive influence is to be detected in general results. I say, then, that the moment Christianity struck the earth, it was evident that a new and astonishing force was in the world—a force affecting the mass of humanity, and not merely a few individuals, a sect, or a nation. Yes, a new force it was that burst as it were from the very core of the world, breaking the old order of things in pieces, dashing down its marble superstitions, injecting a distinct peculiarity among its granitic customs, and leaving a chasm between ancient and modern history. That dividing-line which no eye can miss, is the threshold whence the Kingdom of God began its march through the earth. Since then it has been evident that a moral Power is among men, accomplishing vast and blessed changes. Whatever may have been the specific differences between Athens and Rome for instance, they bear a common resemblance indicating the operation of common ideas. But go forward as many years from the preaching of the Apostles, as backward previous to their mission, and see what a revolution had been wrought in the very heart of society. We may find, perhaps, a less refined literature, less graceful manners, and, on the whole, a ruder civilization—but a far healthier one. A civilization, too, containing a spring of progress, the energy of which we feel to day, and the limit of which we dare not prophecy. We shall find the uncultivated masses, bound by sanctions which the great men of Paganism could not fix, and lifted by a faith which they could not obtain.*

And see what ideas have come down to us since the

*See this argument forcibly illustrated in Volume xiv of "Small Books on Great Subjects," entitled "The state of man before the promulgation of Christianity," p. 3–5.

coming of Christ; ideas whose very *familiarity* constitutes the argument I am now urging. The great doctrine of human brotherhood, of the worth of a man; that he is not to be trod upon as a footstool, or dashed in pieces as a worthless vessel; and the doctrines that grow out of this, the doctrines of popular liberty, education and reform, all these have become active and every-day truths only under the influence of Christianity.

Consider, too, those ideas of religion which breathe around us in the atmosphere of every Sabbath, which consecrate and lift up the humblest congregation—the conceptions of God, of human life, of immortality. How changed is the attitude of men respecting spiritual things! How has this material sphere burst into infinite relations, and the grave lost its terror. How are the guilt and privation of life girdled about with institutions of philanthropy, and its afflictions spanned by the midnight firmament of faith!

But, contrast the general moral aspects of humanity before and since the advent of Christianity, and, moreover, select the most unfavorable point for modern morality. It is a perplexing question whether, as nations advance in refinement, they do not inevitably decline in their moral life. We may inquire, therefore, whether Christianity itself has a conservative influence sufficiently vigorous to prevent its communities from sliding into the worst abominations of Pompeii, or Corinth. In one word, let us take the problem presented by great cities —Paris, London, New-York, and we shall detect, I think, even in such societies, the indications of a moral life far better than the best results of ancient civilization. Think of the *brutality* of those ancient times. Contrast the feelings with which grave senators and chaste women thronged the bloody amphitheatre, with the disgust and indignation which so generally follow the least imitation of such spectacles, at the present day. Well has it been observed, too, that "Christianity has *expurgated* the literature of Greece and Rome." While now immorality is introduced by stealth among the productions of the pen, and these are productions of the meanest sort, how unblushingly did the best minds of old, not only by *permission*, but by *expectation*, blot their pages with filth and vice. If such things are done now, they are not done openly by writers like Catullus or Juvenal. Again, consider how vice now, even when practised, hides itself, is protested against, is repudiated even by the hypocrite who indulges it. Certainly, the respected and the wise condemn it, and such a protest is essential to both their wisdom and their reputation. No one dares approve it, like Cato in the street, or Cicero in the forum. But, above all, our religion confronts such iniquity, wars against it, and moves us to overcome it Can we say this of the religions of antiquity? Can we say this of those who attended a Lupercalian or a Bacchic festival? Even when corruption in modern society is deep, and seems deepening, the true conception remains. There is a moral ideal, a popular standard of virtue, that rebukes this corruption, and that furnishes a recuperative influence.

These, I know, are familiar instances, but I repeat, in the very fact that they are familiar there is a profound indication of the progress which the world has made under the influence of the christian religion. Their familiarity may sometimes deaden their reality to us, and it is well when some local evil, some temporary declension, induces us to despond, to refresh our consciousness of these familiar facts, these general and unmistakeable lineaments of improvement. Thus we shall cherish with new strength our faith in human progress. Amid much evil, mystery, and confusion, we shall detect the calm working of God, and hear the steady march of His Kingdom in the earth, beating like the beating of the world's heart, full of prophecy and full of hope.

III. Let us, *finally*, turn to consider the *essential nature* of this Kingdom. This point has been somewhat anticipated. I have said that the word "Kingdom," as used in the Lord's Prayer, should be translated "*Reign*," and that it indicates a *principle* rather than a *form*, a *spiritual force* rather than a *fixed* and *local* dominion. But this should not lead us into the error of supposing it to be a mere abstraction, a diffused and unorganized influence, a mere sentiment, or philosophy. The Kingdom of God has two characteristics, the one *external*, the other *internal.*

Considered externally, it is an *Historical Fact*, and it has an organized *Form*. It is vitally connected with the Life and Personality of Jesus. It is a progressive principle, but it is not the mere "principle of progress," in the ordinary use of that phrase. It harmonizes with that law of developmeut by which the flower unfolds and the tree grows; it coalesces with that method through which the intellect of man attains its excellence; but it is distinguished from these; it is something more than these. It is not what we usually term a natural law. It springs from a fixed point, it starts from a known era in the world's history, it streams out from the central Personage of the Gospels. I do not mean to say that there were no preparations for it. There were—in the world at large, as well as in the Jewish economy. But I *do* say that these preparations owe their significance to Christ's coming. By his coming, we learn that they *were* preparations. I do say that by him these preliminary elements were first systematized By him they were first concentrated and became a peculiar force, as they were not while isolated. At his coming they were drawn to a focus, brought to bear upon the world, and produced an effect in the world, as never before. As a special law of progress, then—as "the Kingdom of God,"—this spiritual force dates as an historical fact; and from the life and the teachings of Christ, it first begins to leaven the earth and to change its complexion.

Nor should we have built up these great results of the present, by our own unaided effort, and in the natural course of things. This spiritual force, this progressive element, comes to us as a *help* from God—as a special Revelation. We pray to the Father, saying—"*Thy* Kingdom come!" Not ours—not a deliverance we can achieve, an ideal we have wrought. A "Kingdom of *heaven*." Not something we can project from our unguided intuitions, or pluck from the suggestions of science, or from systems of philosophy. Before the advent of Jesus, something was needed by humanity, and sought for, which it could not obtain of itself. It is this desire, this want, that sighs wistfully from the great heart of Heathenism. It is this that heaves up in broken longings from among the symbols of a declining worship. It is this that clouds with dissatisfaction the glory of the oracle, and strips the veil from the beautiful deceits of mythology. It is this that breathes in snatches of fragmentary music, wandering as if in search of the full harmony. It was because of this that Philosophy struggled but could not attain, and the wisest intellects groped among strange splendors and awful shadows. It was this that made the world look at the time Christ came, like a world in eclipse, an exhausted world, a world of orphanage. He filled a great want which until then was unsatisfied. He realized an Ideal, which until then was incomplete. He imparted a power to the soul, which until then it did not possess. Now there is no reason for maintaining that the experience of the past would not be the experience of the present, if Christianity had not appeared. Until its advent there existed this want—at its advent this want is supplied, and new life and new hope inspire mankind. Whatever, therefore, might have been the natural progress of the soul by this time, to that Historical era I point as indicating the period of a special influence—a time to which men once looked forward and to which they now defer. Judging by the past, I contend that without that Revelation we should not stand on the high ground we now occupy. And, if I am told that the present stage of human progress is a natural development, I say—not so. There has evidently been a wonderful and peculiar crisis in the history of the race. If intellect and affection, if intuition and sentiment could have achieved this profound moral life and this firm, transcendant faith, why did they not do so before Christ? Were there not then as noble hearts, and as colossal intellects as now? Did not these intuitions work as curiously, did not reason seek as ardently for truth? Did not the moral nature gravitate as spontaneously towards an ideal virtue? Did not Love mourn as tenderly over the graves of the dead? If, then, this high faith, this spiritual life, are merely natural developments, why not known before? But am I referred to our advantages, that did not surround those ancient minds? Yet, whence the spring of all these advantages? Yes, we have advantages that the good and the wise of old had not—even that living WORD that was made known to the world, eighteen hundred years ago. Or, once more, is it said that Christianity itself, although a great propelling force, is a natural product of circumstances—that the very wants and desires to which I have alluded, engendered it? With more reason should we say, that it was an adaptation to those wants—that it did not spring from them, but descended to meet them. I repeat, then, that, while I do not deny the kindly helps of nature, and the intrinsic revelations of the human soul, Christianity is something more than these, and the Kingdom of God could not have been built up without its peculiarity. It is an Historical Religion—an organized system of Truth—a Personal embodiment of Righteousness, which Kings and Prophets desired to see, but did not; which *we* see, and which gives a specific definition and a concrete character to the Kingdom of heaven.

But this Kingdom is also *internal,* and, having sufficiently guarded against misapprehension, I observe, that chiefly, essentially, it is spiritual, and is in the human soul. Christ emphatically declared that "it comes not with observation." The Jew was waiting for some outward display. He expected a material revelation of this kingdom. That it would come as with a whirlwind, breaking the cedars of Lebanon—that it would advance as with the tramp of armies, shaking Cesar on his throne—that it would descend manifestly from heaven—that it would hover in mystic glory above the temple. And yet, even while the Scribes and Pharisees were looking for it, lo! it *had* come, and he who introduced it told them it was among them. It was felt rather than seen, and yet to a discerning eye it was manifest in the absorbed attention of the multitude, and the new powers of the disciples. It had come in a strange energy, breathing over the sea of Galilee and among the leaves of Olivet. He did not strive nor cry, and yet when his cross was reared its throne was already set up; when his Apostles went forth with their message its dominion had commenced. No custom had yielded, no institution was abolished, yet calmly that force was developing itself which should change the world's aspect, and regenerate the world's heart—before which idolatries should crumble and empires pass away. It was a *spiritual* power. Its seat was in the human heart—its conquest was over the human soul.

Yet, even now, it is to be apprehended, that men but crudely understand the spiritual nature of this Kingdom—that still they too much regard it as outward and future, too little as present and universal. Let me say, then, that this Kingdom of heaven for which we pray, is neither a ceremonial nor a territory, it is not mere deliverance from social wrongs or from outward evils, it is not merely the blessedness of the immortal world, or the millenial epoch. It is all these—it comprehends these; it may be manifested in these various phases—but primarily, essentially, it is not these. It is simply Holiness, Truth, and Love; and when we pray "Thy Kingdom come!" we pray that it may descend into, regenerate, and dwell in our hearts and in all hearts. It is not meat and drink, but "righteousness, and peace, and joy in the Holy Ghost." I would that we might realize this truth, for it would prevent many errors in thought and conduct. It would teach us how and where to look for its indications. It would impress us with a sense of our *indivi dual agency* and our *individual responsibility,* in regard to this Kingdom. When our own hearts come under the control of Divine affections, and are moved by holy aspirations; when Divine truth is clear to our minds, and we are obedient to its dictates, then is that prayer answered for ourselves—then for us has that Kingdom come.

And as to the advancement of that Kingdom through the world, let us cherish no conceptions which are calculated to discourage our exertions, or to induce an indolent fatalism. Let us not expect that it will come suddenly and irresistibly, without patience and labor. Let us not dwell too much upon the social aspects and the material splendors of this Kingdom. Nor should we obscure the true idea of this consummation even with the glories of heaven. It is true, we cannot fix a limit to the whole idea which is involved in the prayer of the text. We cannot say how much is external, and how much is internal in that desired condition, or to what degree the blessedness of heaven mingles with the possibilities of earth. But again I say, let us remember that however, or wherever that consummation may appear, it is essentially a state of the soul—it expresses the bliss and excellence of holy and loving spirits, and no material figures can adequately symbolize it.

And now, my friends, as I bring these remarks to a

close, I cannot help observing the peculiar appropriateness of our theme to the present condition of the world. It is a time of universal agitation, and of momentous interest. It is an age of gigantic materialism. On every hand, science is penetrating the domain of matter, and subduing its essence to the human will; while the lust of gold is fed by the discovery of treasure richer than the dreams of fiction. It is an age, too, of controversy and experiment, of the profoundest questionings and the most critical issues. The genius of Reform, whether we call it by a good, or a bad name, wrestles with established power, the spirit of innovation stirs the most sluggish veins, and the torch of investigation flares in the face of all authority. In fine, as never before, it seems as if the great conflict between good and evil, the trial whether material or spiritual interests shall predominate, were, for a long time to come at least, to be decided. Who, then, can be indifferent to the decision? Who amid this upspringing of material interests, this fall of dynasties, this activity of intellectual and moral forces, will not continually utter the prayer of the text? If, then, we understand its meaning; if we are honestly conscious that it is to be fulfilled by our labor as well as our supplications; if we would realize it in our own souls and have it extend to the souls of others; if we trust in the glorious promise which it implies; if we heartily desire that great consummation ; let us wrestle with it in the secrecy of the closet, let us lift it amid the busy and contending principles of the world ; let us breathe it through the dead formalities of religion—for never was it needed more!

DISCOURSE IV.

"Thy will be done in earth as it is in heaven."—Matthew vi: 10.

THE Christian conception of man's relation to God, involves two ideas—*Dependence* and *Obedience.* We live, move, and have our being, in an all-comprehending Spirit, apart from which we could no more exist than drops separated from the fountain. He who controls the mechanism of nature, touches all the springs of our life. His constant force sustains us, and His irresistible ordinances engird us. We are the creatures of Infinite Power and the pensioners of exhaustless Goodness. Thus, human nature, considered by itself, appears incompetent. It instinctively leans upon something higher. And in the consciousness of dependence, thus manifest, in the soul, philosophers detect a universal intuition of the Deity.

Yet, with this consciousness, mingles another—that of spiritual affinity to the Creator. We know that we are not merely His creatures, but His offspring. We share his nature. And the glory of that nature is *moral freedom*—power to act or to resist, to choose or to reject. So, although as finite existences we hang upon the Infinite, although as material creatures we are held in an irresistible control, as spiritual beings we have a sphere of our own, a realm of voluntary action. Into this circle, God does not intrude His absolute Power, but His intrinsic Righteousness. He does not *force* it, but He *appeals* to it. He does not bind its service as the Omnipotent Maker, but demands its free allegiance as the Moral Governor. And if, as we have seen, on the one hand, the human soul assumes the attitude of incompleteness and reliance; on this, it evinces a consciousness of liberty, a conviction of power, a feeling of obligation. And if, moreover, the general instinct of dependence proves the existence of a God, as profound a proof appears in this universal moral sense—this idea of obedience. And these ideas, I repeat, Christianity blends. If we are truly imbued with its spirit, we cannot separate them. They form one conception; and the sentiment with which we regard the Deity is at once one of reverence and of love, of prayer and homage, of responsibility and resignation.

I speak now of the *practical* conclusion to which Christianity brings us. Back of this, there is a question of immemorial controversy—the question between God's sovereignty and man's agency. But, I repeat, the practical conclusion to which our Religion brings us—the conclusion upon which we spontaneously act, and from which we live every day—the mood of mind, in short, with which we breathe the prayer of the text, is not prevented by this question. Whatever logical inconsistency may be detected in our sentiments, and debated upon at other times, when we come before God, we combine the ideas of dependence and obedience. Feeling that there is a wide sphere in which He acts irresistibly, we also feel that there is a wide sphere in which He is not served; and so, with a mingled desire, we pray—"Thy Will be done!"

And yet, though, while using the general expressions of the prayer, we combine these sentiments, there are special seasons when one will be more prominent in our souls than another, and may even for a time glow exclusively there; and for either we shall find the language of the text a proper vehicle. We may utter it as a sentiment of ***Resignation***, or as a sentiment of ***Responsibility***. A consideration of these two conditions will naturally distribute my remarks under two heads.

I. I observe, then, that there are circumstances which peculiarly quicken our sense of *dependence*. When we go out into the material universe, and consider its manifestations of infinite Power, a Power which, being central and diffusive, ordains both variety and harmony, projects these enormous forces, and secures this beautiful order; when we consider the range of its influence and the minuteness of its touch—how sublimely great masses obey its dictates, and with what alacrity each little pipe and valve fulfils its part, and yet, while tides change and planets turn, how calmly the great circle spins its diligent task; and then, when we consider that our being also hangs upon the fiat of this universal Controller—that the Eye which looks through all this complexity, numbers the hairs of our head—that the Presence which shows itself in this great accordance, glances upon us in the light and wraps us with the wind; in such a mood of the soul, feeling peculiarly the pressure of the Divine Power, and yet ardently conscious, also, that it is a Power of Order, Beneficence, and Beauty, we think of nothing but our dependence as a part of the stupendous mechanism; we lean back upon the mighty whole; we utter a devout ejaculation in harmony with the general current of things; we pour, as it were, our glad consent in among these fluent necessities of nature, and exclaim—"Thy Will be done!"

Again, there are times when the elements around us break out in appalling manifestations. The earthquake overturns the dwellings of men, and the volcano blasts their vineyards. The ship goes down at sea, and the agonized cry of hundreds is unheard amid the roar of the tempest and the dash of the billows. The Pestilence marches across the earth like an invisible host, beleagures nations and decimates cities. Famine haunts the hearth-stone and the threshold, and broods in the empty corn-fields! The very forces whose serene order inspires us with admiration, and whose bountiful provisions supply our wants, thus become agents of ruin and dismay. We are overtaken by a conviction of weakness. Evidently, a Hand far stronger than our own, is unbinding the secret powers or checking the ordinary currents of nature. We can neither command nor escape them. Our art is baffled, and we must yield. And then, if our faith is firm and clear, the ejaculation in the text will appropriately leap from our hearts.

Or some more private affliction has smitten us. Some well-wrought plan has been disappointed. Our promise is killed, our hope is put out. We find that we have leaned upon a reed, and it has broken and pierced us. Sickness, perhaps, has surprised us in the midst of many cares. Or, notwithstanding all our diligence, poverty has come upon us "like an armed man." Or our tenderest affections have been touched and torn. We have stood by some new-made grave. We have consigned some dear form to the dust. We have returned to the house of mourning, and for the first time have realized the emptiness and the desolation of our home. And again we are oppressed by a sense of utter weakness—of a mysterious Power that disposes of us and our circumstances—a Power that we cannot hinder. And, if the depth of our grief is qualified by genuine submission, if our agony is wrung from a filial heart, there are no words so fitted for us as the words now before us.

Here, then, or in other conditions of human life that might be suggested, there is forced upon us a profound sense of dependence, and of dependence upon God alone. For the things in which we usually trust, and upon which we confidingly lean, are plucked from us. Our skill is baffled, our power is as a straw, and those in whom we had garnered our affections, and who seemed to us a shelter from the inclemency of the world, are cut down and leave us alone. Dependence, I repeat, and dependence upon the Infinite only, is the great conviction which oversweeps us, and we may well say—what else *can* we say?—"Thy Will be done!"

But, I remark further, if we breathe this prayer intelligently, we do not contemplate mere Power; we do not separate the Omnipotence of God from the rest of His Attributes. We consider to *Whose* will we submit. Nor must we confound His Will with His *Sovereignty*. His sovereignty is His absolute control. His will is the *disposition* with which He wields that control. Power is but the instrument, Will is the intention which wields the instrument. Power is not a moral quality. As has been shown in a previous discourse, it may command our awe and our admiration, but of itself it cannot claim our worship. When we pray—"Thy Will be done," then, we must have reference to the character of the Deity; to His Wisdom, Justice, and Goodness, as well as His Power. Otherwise, the ejaculation is slavishness not true worship. It is a forced acquiescence, not a devout desire. The Christian always regards the *moral significance* unfolded in every display of God's supremacy, and in all His workings. In one word, he recognizes God in all. But the man who sees only the power and not the intention; who says "Thy Will be done," because he must, without discrimination as to *whose* will it is, or *what* it is, hardly feels, in any sense, the sentiment of the text. He would express the same acquiescence if there were no God—if he were chained to the wheel of destiny, and driven by the blind forces of nature.

In close connection with this error, and, in fact a modification of the same principle, is that *fatalism* which translates "Thy Will be done," into an excuse for indolence and neglect. Doubtless, there are many who assume the attitude of pious resignation without the sentiment. They cast upon Providence the burden of their own follies and sins. The sluggard mourns over his barren fields, and says—"Thy Will be done!" "Thy Will be done!" exclaims the improvident man entangled among the miseries of poverty. And he who has carelessly strained the laws of his physical being, and lies wasting to death, utters the same devout language. But let us understand that *fatalism,* whether it assume the form of torpid acquiescence, or of inconsiderate reliance, is not *resignation.* It is right to recognize an overruling Providence, but it is a Providence that works *with* us, not *for* us. The impatience with which we beat the walls of difficulty and heave against misfortune, is not an impious discontent, but a spring of noble enterprise, which God encourages, for which He has opened a wide sphere of action, and by which alone we can achieve success. To suppose that He prevents this effort, is to suppose that He infringes His own ordinances established for the wisest and most benevolent ends. To attribute calamity to Him without making this effort, is to confound faith with folly,and religion with laziness. Only by the diligent exertion of our own will, can we realize the Will of God mysteriously working with us. Only when we have reached the boundary of our extremest effort, can we see the superior purpose which encircles us. Only when we have done all we can, and plainly perceive that the current of a mightier, a wiser and a better Will sets against ours and sways things otherwise, only then springs up within us a vivid consciousnence of *dependence,* only then breaks from our lips a sincere prayer of resignation.

We see, then, that under a consciousness of human weakness, it is a great thing to say—" Thy Will be done!" To say it not in sullen acquiescence, not in indolent reliance, not in formal mockery. To say it when our best hopes are breaking, when the dearest objects are plucked away, when our hearts are wrung with loss, and disappointment, and suspense. A great thing to say it profoundly, out from depths of our nature that are stirred with wonder and with agony. To say it with the full force of our souls. To say it while our tears are falling in the light of religious trust. It is a great thing, too, to know *why* we say it, and what we mean by it; nay, we cannot truly utter it without we do know. We cannot rightly say it without an intelligent perception of God. Only when the expressions that stand before it in the Lord's Prayer, are known by us not as an accidental succession of sentences in a formula but as the natural unfolding of a spiritual experience, can we really breathe the sentiment of the text. Only when with an understanding mind, and a heartfelt desire, we have said—" Our Father which art in heaven, hallowed be thy name, thy Kingdom come;" only then can we sincerely say—" Thy Will be done."

II. But, passing to the second division of my discourse, I remark, that we may employ the words of the text when quickened by the sense of *Responsibility*. The prayer is not merely one of resigned acquiescence, but of earnest desire. To repeat what I said in the outset, we utter this petition feeling that not only is there a wide sphere in which God acts irresistibly, but also there is a wide sphere in which He is not served. It is in reference to the last, that I speak under this head. Turning from the field of nature, where God's control is so apparent; turning from those resistless mysteries of life that mingle with the experience of us all and fill us with a vivid consciousness of dependence; we find a world in which His Will is not completely done. It is the world of man's moral nature, and of his moral action. I do not intend to embarass myself with the controversy to which I alluded in the commencement of this discourse—the question between the sovereignty of God and the free-agency of man. Mere logic cannot settle the dispute; for it demonstrates one side just as much as the other; or at least, in the controversy, logic is met by an authority equally legitimate. That authority is our own *moral sense.* We are conscious of a will, independent and personal. In this we find a strong demonstration of the existence of a God. For the experience of a will in ourselves, renders us capable of detecting the indications of another and a Divine Will in the works of the universe. The experience of the independent personality of our own will, enables us to confirm the independent personality of God's Will—that He is not one with his creation—that we are separate beings from Him. The existence of His sovereignty, too, of His infinite will, is proved by a process of argument that legitimates our own sovereignty, however limited that sovereignty may be—its freedom in a certain sphere, however narrow that sphere. Knowing that *He* is a mind from the fact that we are minds,—we also know that a distinguishing characteristic of mind is moral freedom, power of choice and action, a sense of right and wrong. This separates it from matter—this separates man from the brute. If, then, we have the essential prerogatives of mind, and if we are separate minds from the Deity, we may act counter to God's Will.

But not only does consciousness suggest that we may act counter to God's will, it assures us that we *do* thus act. No man, however *logically* he may have arrived at the conclusion that he sins by God's adamantine decree, that he is fated to be wicked, fails to feel rebuked when he *does* sin. Conscience mutters its thunder against the wrong, and a sense of retribution opens in his soul. But why the indignant remonstrance, why the foreboding fear, if he has done only what he was *obliged* to do? Say what he will, his moral nature, as authentic and as infallible as his intellect, assures him by its rebuke that he had a power of choice, and that having freely chosen the wrong he must pay the penalty of his election.

But, not protracting discussion, I assume from the language of the text, that God's will is *not* done, offering the views which I have just given as an interpretation of that language. In the moral world, in the world of man's own power and action, however we may explain it, evidently there is a profound sense in which that will is not obeyed. I have spoken of the occasional outbreak of material elements—of the tempest, the pestilence, and the volcano. But, after all, from whence come the worst desolations in the earth?—what are the most fearful wrecks we see? Are not man's passions more fierce than the elements? Are not the ruin and dismay they cause, more dreadful? Are not the spectacles which sicken our souls the most; which most trouble the faith of the Christian, and perplex the labors of the philanthropist; those which have come from the workings of the human will, and out from the doors of the human heart?

While, in bowing to the irresistible evils of our lot, the human soul frequently illustrates its dignity, in yielding to evils that it might resist, and that spring from its own depths, it exposes its weakness and its shame. And while from the desolations of the material universe—from the torn mountain, the earthquake's wrinkles, the scars of the tempest—come rich suggestions of sublimity and beauty, how striking, often, is the contrast between the aspects of nature and the world that man makes! Sunny lands overspread with indolence and vice; fair cities, whose splendors are tarnished by steams of corruption; while the morning and the night look down upon crimes that mock their loveliness and insult their purity. See how another force, different from and counter to that power upon which we all depend, prevails in the earth! That human form, so skillfully fashioned but now marred by *intemperance*; the loathsome flesh, the trembling limbs, the silly stare, the unhinged reason, the gibbering speech, the imbruited man—*this* is not the work of nature, this is no irresistible fatality; it is the expression of a human will that has surrendered to appetite, and that is consumed by lust. Enter some haunt of infamy, and looking with pure and sad eyes below all the tawdry glitter, the sensual show, ponder the wreck and desolation there! Humanity, garnished with its own shame, and laughing at its own sacrifice! Jaded beauty bronzed too hard to blush; art lending the blushes that abused nature will not give! The crown of womanhood cast down, and the wealth of her affections transmuted to iniquity and deceit. And yet, beneath those frivolous blandishments, what broken memories of good still linger, what a dreary sense of loss, what utter misery! And, if we could uncoil the windings of the heart that first projected this result; if we could read the soul of the tempter who betrayed confiding love, and balanced virtue against needed gold, or bread; truly, my friends, we should realize that there is a will in the world, working fearfully, which is *not* God's Will!

Or if, turning from forms of evil which open upon us in saloons and cellars, we look out upon wider theatres of human action, how appalling are the spectacles that meet us! I will detain you, however, for illustration, with only one, and this I cannot forego. It is so familiar and yet so striking; it shows so forcibly how much man's passions have marred man's condition, and, as I have said, how deep is the contrast, often, between the work he does, and the universe in which he lives.

Stand, then, in imagination, of a summer's morning, upon a field of battle. Earth and sky melt together in light and harmony. The air is rich with fragrance, and sweet with the song of birds. But, suddenly, breaks in the sound of fiercer music, and the measured tramp of thousands. Eager squadrons shake the earth with thunder, and files of bristling steel kindle in the sun. And opposed to each other, line to line, face to face, are now arrayed men whom God has made in the same likeness, and whose nature He has touched to the same issues. The same heart beats in all. In the momentary hush, like a swift mist sweep before them images of home. Voices of children prattle in their ears, Memories of affection stir among their silent prayers. They cherish the same sanctities, too. They have read from the same Book. It is to them the same charter of life and salvation. They have been taught to observe its beautiful lessons of love. Their hearts have been touched alike with the meek Example of Jesus. But a moment —and all these affinities are broken, trampled under foot, swept away by the shock and the shouting. Confusion rends the air. The simmering bomb ploughs up the earth. The iron hail cuts the quivering flesh. The steel bites to the bone. The cannon-shot crashes through serried ranks. And under a cloud of smoke that hides both earth and heaven, the desperate struggle goes on. The day wanes, and the strife ceases. On the one side there is a victory, on the other a defeat. The triumphant city is lighted with jubilee, the streets roll out their tides of acclamation, and the organ heaves from its groaning breast the peal of thanksgiving. But, under that tumultuous joy, there are bleeding bosoms and inconsolable tears. And, whether in triumphant or defeated lands, a shudder of orphanage and widowhood, a chill of wo and death runs far and wide through the world. The meek moon breaks the dissipating vail of the conflict, and rolls its calm splendor above the dead. And see now how much wo man has mingled with the inevitable evils of the universe! See now the fierceness of his passion, the folly of his wickedness, witnessed by the torn standards, the broken wheels, the pools of clotted blood, the charred earth, the festering heaps of slain. Nature did not make these horrors, and, when those fattening bones shall have mouldered in the soil, she will spread out luxuriant harvests, to hide those horrors forever.

No, my friends, the moral world, the world of man's action, is not in harmony with the Will of God. The earth, like a huge whispering-gallery, reverberates with echoes of unnecessary wo. There peal the sighs of unrelieved want, the protests of abused confidence, the prayer that bursts from the middle-passage of the slave-ship, the clank of chains rising from fields of oppression. Reason as we will, there is that within us that shrinks from attributing this to the desire of the infinite Father. At least, there is that which urges us with a strong conviction of need—with a strong conviction of discord and evil—to breathe earnestly the prayer—"Thy Will be done!"

This, then, I conceive to be another mode of applying the words of the text. With a sense of responsibility resting in man, we pray that the moral evils in the world may pass away, that humanity may be changed to peace and holiness—may become one with God. Looking out upon the wide earth, with the glorious prospect of what it may be contrasted with what it is—of light and harmony, of righteousness and joy, taking the place of all this sin and wo, we lift the fervent petition before us.

And yet, while implicating ourselves with all this, we likewise refer to something out of ourselves. We distinctly recognize a Will working *with* us. We feel that a Power far mightier than our own, mingles with the issues of the moral world. I would not present the arena of human action in too gloomy an aspect. I would not hide the horizon of promise that glows around it. If God does not ordain evil He resists it, and in the conflict the good is stronger than the bad. Nor would I urge any doctrine which makes the moral universe a chaos and an uncertainty. Let us cherish faith in an overruling Providence in history, and in individual circumstances. Those men who have accomplished the most; who have left their mark in the world, and given an impulse to future ages, have always cherished this high faith in a sovereign rule and an appointed destiny.

But I do urge that we should likewise be true to our own consciousness which asserts our free-agency, and that we find that point in moral action where the indications of an overruling Providence harmonize with the idea of human responsibility. And especially do I ask you to consider the individual application of this prayer. We pray that God's will may be done. But do *we* do it —do you and I strive to accomplish it? Let us not confine our attention to the aspects of the world at large. Let each look into his own heart. How is that? Is there no moral dislocation—no resistance to God's will there? Are we reconciled to Him? If not, then we shall, of all things, strive and pray, seeking for His spiritual help, His working in us, until our will becomes one with His. This, indeed, is the most intense, the most necessary application of all. Without this, whatever else we may profess or do, our prayer is insincere.

I have now shown how the Prayer of the text is appropriate for either of the conceptions involved in our relations to God—appropriate as an expression of dependence, and as a desire for obedience. But while I have exhibited the accordance of the petition with these two facts; or, rather, have shown that these two facts are harmonized in the prayer; let me remind you, in closing, that in the text itself we have an interpretation of its meaning. "Thy will be done in earth *as it is in heaven!* To what do we refer here by the term "*Heaven?*" Do we mean the material firmament, the starry canopy above our heads? The reference is appropriate even if this *is* our meaning. For how beautifully is God's Will done by those revolving spheres, those bright and circling systems? A common influence binds them; and how diligent their obedience, how peaceful their motions, how calmly the eternal law shines out from them through all the changing years! And do we pray that thus we and all men, may move in harmony each with each, and all with God? That thus we may obey, and feel the beating of his influence, the current of His consent mingling eternally with ours? So may it be then, if we take this material order merely as an *illustration*. But if we mean more than this—if we would see not only an illustration but the result itself, then, when we say "as in heaven," we must look higher. For, surely, we are not mere masses of matter; machines moved only by a foreign touch, and propelled upon the orbit of an inflexible destiny. We are *spirits*, we are moral, we are free! And if we would behold the ideal result of this prayer, then we must look into the *spiritual* heaven, the abode of angelic hosts, and of "the just made perfect." "Let thy will be done, O God!" we should say, "as it is *there*—in the heaven of spiritual order but of voluntary obedience; where every will is free, yet is in unison with thine." That heaven whose glory is the consciousness in each of a self-balanced power gravitating to the Infinite Centre of all. Where the bliss of each is to *be* like the will that each *does*. Let thy will be done, O God! harmoniously, as in the material, freely, as in the spiritual heaven. The convulsed and groaning earth sends up the cry—our erring, guilty hearts send up the cry—"Let thy will be done in earth, as it is done far above these sins and sorrows, in the realm of obedience and joy, of perpetual worship and perpetual action, of boundless peace and boundless love!"

DISCOURSE V.

"Give us this day our daily bread."—Matthew vi: 11.

Although, as has been shown, individual reference is *implied* in preceding sentences of this Prayer, the text is the first in which personal supplication is actually *expressed.* The foregoing petitions are more largely qualified by the sentiment of *homage,* this contains more specially the sentiment of *desire.* When we pray that God's Name may be hallowed, or His Kingdom come, or His Will be done, we virtually pray that *we* may hallow His name, that His kingdom may be established in *our* souls; that His will may be accomplished through the harmonious consent of *our* natures with His. Yet, these may be uttered as *ejaculations,* breathed in the posture of worship, general aspirations kindled by a contemplation of God's glory, and only after reflection, drawn down and applied to our personal wants and duties. But the prayer of the text, is, as it were, forced out by the pressure of immediate necessities, and lifted as a stringent desire. In the consciousness not only of

God's Power and Excellence, but of our human weakness and solicitous need, we cry—"Give us this day our daily bread!"

As another introductory remark, it may be well to say that the main points involved in the last discourse are again brought before us by the text, although here they have a different reference. If, then, this fact should occasion some similarity of ideas, I trust that these ideas may be more vividly impressed upon your minds by variety of illustration.

With these preliminary considerations, let us now proceed to discuss the spirit of this petition, the meaning which we should attach to it, the way in which we can consistently use it. In other words, let us dwell upon some suggestions which spring from the language of the text.

I. The words before us, show that *earthly interests and animal wants have an appropriate place in our prayers.* Perhaps it is not too much to say, that, among religionists of almost every class, there is a tendency to undervalue, and even to despise, our material existence, and the facts with which it is peculiarly connected. There is a habit of speaking of the earth in which we live, and the body through which we act, that, as a mere expression of the comparative value of sensual and spiritual things, is not justifiable. Though "spiritual interests *are* real and supreme," material interests are not entirely unworthy. But, while there are some in whom the opposite tendency breaks out with a manichean hatred of the flesh, or in ascetic mortifications, now a few who regard these extremes as superstitious, nay, who would repudiate the very tendency to which I now allude, still seem to fancy that it is peculiarly religious to contemn our animal nature, to paint this mortal scene in hues of gloom and vanity, and to contemplate death with ardent desire and with rapturous welcome. This sentiment unconsciously influences their religious feelings, and colors their religious views. But this sentiment, it seems to me, indicates confused spiritual perceptions, and positively injures spiritual interests. We not only give an undue exaltation to the appetites when we yield them a blind service, but when we concentrate upon them a microscopic *surveillance*. It is a grave idea of heaven to conceive it as one set of external circumstances, which we attain by escaping from another set here below. It is a crude religiousness which seeks to glorify the future life by depreciating this, or that villifies the body in order to exalt the soul. It is a great mistake to confound exstatic feelings, and super-mundane moods, with essential righteousness. And, after all, the man who realizes the supremacy of spiritual things, is he who perceives the value of material things, and who, by a comprehensive vision and a fresh experience, knows their mutual offices, and the clear line of demarcation between the two. The body is not essentially vile: it is marred by our passions, and, having broken down the fences of the soul, we yield to evil suggestions which steal in through its agency. But it is the intricate and beautiful workmanship of God, the consummate evidence of His skill, and the instrument of countless blessings. The earth though often called "a den of wickedness," and "a vale of tears," is not wholly so. It is a world which the Creator has adorned with loveliness and filled with wonder. If *we will*, it may prove to us a porch of knowledge, a temple of devotion, and a noble theatre of duty. Life is to be cherished as a sacred thing; health is to be cared for as a precious gift; in short, the means of temporal welfare are to be sought and preserved as a religious duty—for, in our holiest moods, in our prayers, we are instructed to say—"Give us this day our daily bread."

But, while it may be necessary to say thus much against an unconscious asceticism, it is, undoubtedly, far more necessary to state the proposition I am now discussing in its application to a tendency exactly the opposite of this—the tendency to absorption in the earthly life, and in material interests. This is a result far more widely-extended than the other, and, therefore, in opposition to this, I repeat—that earthly interests and animal wants, have an *appropriate* place in this prayer —an *appropriate* place among our highest and most serious thoughts. Appropriate, my friends, because they hold a *secondary* place. The text is the only petition in the Lord's Prayer in which the desire for *temporal* good is directly expressed. The rest is for the coming of God's Kingdom, and the doing of His Will; for forgiveness of sin, and for deliverance from temptation. And this small space allotted to earthly aspirations is appropriate, because thus is expressed the *comparative* value of material and spiritual interests. And yet, is this the practical estimate which men generally set upon the two? Is it *this* that is expressed in the diligence and solicitude of this busy hive—the world?

But, not to dwell upon the daily pursuits and the ordinary desires of the many—how is it even with their *prayers?* Is not the main current of their petitions a desire for *earthly* good? Are not their profoundest regrets stirred by *material* losses and evils? Are not their thanksgiving chiefly inspired by *sensual* ease and plenty? This thanksgiving, this regret, this petition, is all well enough, if it only occupies its appropriate place —if its intensity is duly qualified. But if *spiritual* needs, losses, blessings are forgotten, or faintly mentioned, surely our devotions are not after the model of the

Lord's Prayer. And surely, my friends, we thus betray our deepest wishes and our highest ideals. We show how sensual is our notion of good, and our view of life. And how many are there here to-night, whose wishes and conceptions are thus characterized?—who, if they should wring out the most subtile aspiration of their hearts, if they should embody the fondest ideal that brightens over them, if they should delineate the image that hope and desire paint upon their future, would show us a representation of mere earthly good; health, ease, plenty, friends, fame, pleasure; with a nebulous ring of moral conception encircling all, and a vague notion of heaven sparkling afar off! How do such regards, I say, animate the profoundest prayers of the many! This should not be so, O man! This should not be your relative estimate of spiritual and material things. I have shown that these material interests have their value, and their office, and a place in our religion; but let them not have the supreme place, because, comparatively, they are brief and shallow, while spiritual interests are deep and permanent. That material ideal, even if realized, cannot satisfy you. That sensual object, even if attained, will be merely touched by you, and then must slip from you forever. "The fashion of this world passeth away," but, quicker even than *that* vanishing, your voice among its multitudes will be still, your footsteps will be effaced from its bosom, and its vernal greenness will spring from your very ashes. Ask and seek for your daily bread, then; but remember that it is "the bread that perisheth," and that "man shall not live by bread alone, but by every word that proceedeth out of the mouth of God."

II. The next fact which I would dwell upon as suggested by the text, is the truth of our *intimate dependence upon God.* The light in which I would now urge this truth, is somewhat different from the illustration employed in the last discourse. I spoke then of the sense of dependence forced upon us by extraordinary revelations in nature, and by peculiar crises in life. But is it not too generally the fact that this consciousness of dependence is awakened only by unusual circumstances? Is it not too much the case, that we recognise God only in the whirlwind and the flame? What I wish to urge under this head, then, is that we should *constantly* realize our dependence upon the Deity—that we should habitually and sincerely acknowledge Him as the source of all our good. With clear faith and spontaneous emotion, we should own that our most minute and ordinary blessings, the air, the sunshine, our *daily bread,* come from Him. No truth is more trite than this. This, probably, was one of the first sentences of the Lord's Prayer that we were able to comprehend. Perhaps the earliest conception of God that dawned upon our infant minds, was that of the "Great Giver," who bestows our shelter, our raiment, our food; and, impressed by this idea, we have knelt down, and, with our little, childish voices, prayed—"Give us this day our daily bread." But it is to be feared that we do not carry this simple faith into our maturer years. Ask almost any man, if he believes in the existence of a God, and he says—"Yes." Ask him if he believes that God is the Creator of all things, and nothing will he more readily affirm. Ask him if he believes that He is the great Benefactor, and gratefully will he acknowledge it. And yet, is it not a fact that, with a vast number, this belief exists merely as a logical conclusion, a traditional creed, or a fitful confession of the heart, and that, in reality, they are *practical* atheists? Do they not, *virtually*, consider something else than God as the source of their blessings? Is He not lost sight of, is He not put out of view—as the Maker who has left the machine, as the Creator who is hidden by His works? Nay, *plenty* itself, the most profuse evidence of God, is often that which most shuts us in from Him. In the blasted harvest and the unfruitful year, perhaps, we fall upon our knees, and think of *His* agency who retains the shower and veils the sun. But when the wheels of nature roll on their accustomed course, when our fields are covered with sheaves and our garners groan with abundance, we may lift a transient offering of gratitude; yet, in the continuous flow of prosperity, are we not apt to refer largely to our own enterprise, and bless our "*luck?*" Do we not virtually do this, rather than realize that the Almighty hand has touched all these issues, and that without His constant action there would be nothing? In other words, does God meet us in all these results? Do we regard them as fresh creations of His power and goodness? Do we entertain a vivid sense of an actual and immediate Providence? I repeat, we are apt to regard merely *secondary* causes, to glorify our own power and skill, and, in the customary flow of success, to feel but faintly our constant dependence upon the great Giver.

Perhaps *science* nourishes this error. Revealing to us the constant operation of material laws, it begets a tendency to deify those laws, to transmute them from theoretical equivalents into absolute realities, to conceive them as rigid statutes rather than flexible expressions of the Infinite will. It is hard for us to believe that God instantly creates; we expect the production gradually, through some process. Yet, what is that process but a creation at each point, inspired by His moving spirit and seized by His intention? Is the *living power* of God absent from the ascending vapor and the bursting seed?

Does not the up-gathering of the one, the unfolding of the other, indicate His instant presence and the steady pressure of His hand, as much as the finished flower, or the planet? If, then, we erect these natural laws into rigid forms that intercept God's contact with His works, if we consider them as God, practically, we are atheists. And we are perplexed by all the vagueness and inconsistency of atheism; for we do not account for these laws themselves—we do not define them. If we did, we should see that they are but established ways of God's working, the unseen arteries of His will; the fluent methods of His Beneficence and His Power; and that our daily bread, every grain of wheat, whatever its secondary dependencies and introductory processes, is direct from Him.

And yet, there is a repugnance to admit the doctrine of an instant Providence, not only from a false reverence for natural laws, but because such a notion, as some think, seems unworthy of the Deity. That He should create a universe, that He should control the general concerns of being, appears in some degree fitted to His Majesty. But that He should touch with His own hand our daily supplies, and dispose the essentials of our individual lot, seems too minute for Him. I cannot share this feeling. If my admiration is kindled by contemplating the scale of God's operation, the vastness and splendor of His works, surely my reverence is increased, my love is heightened, when I notice, also, the extent to which that creation descends, the small details which it involves, the delicacy as well as the magnitude of His Government. To borrow the illustration of Chalmers, I lift the *telescope,* and my wonder is inflamed when it sweeps the glittering fields of space, and multiplies the starry legions of the firmament. But when I take up the *microscope,* and discover the myriad-fold existence that is hidden from the naked eye, the swarming joy that populates a drop, and find the atom endowed with eyes to see, and nerves to feel, and surrounded by its universe of glory too, my wonder deepens to worship, and the conception of an *infinite* God more clearly breaks upon me. To realize, then, that He whom the angels cannot fully know, mingles His Presence with our common walks, and hears and answers the widow's cry for bread, seems to me the most appropriate faith for a truly devout soul.

But, whatever may be the hindrance to our conception of an ever-present and ever-acting Deity, and to a vivid sense of our continual dependence upon Him, it may all be comprehended in this one word—*custom.* We are startled into a belief in His Providence by extraordinary events, but it is hidden from us by usual circumstances. Our keen sense of Him is muffled by familiarity. In the flow of material things we drift away from the thought of Him. The obedient operation of our own faculties, unhinges our faith in the infinite Power. The intrusiveness of man's works, shuts out the evidence of God's works. The pomp of scientific demonstration cheats us. But, if we would abandon the populous city, the book and the crucible, the implements of labor and the garden of plenty, and go out into the wilderness, and, in child-like renunciation of our theories, contemplate some flower that blooms there all alone; think *how* it came, *what* ordained it, and what secret life courses its tiny veins; ask how it sprung from the unconscious sod; think of the mystery that lies at its root, and breathes in its fragrant life—we may waken to some conception of the mystery that is also in and around us—of not only the final but the immediate dependence of all things upon a higher and all-controlling Power. Nay, if, not waiting for sickness, or disappointment, or death, in the silence of meditation we will consider our real dependence; will ask how and by what we live; who holds the links of our being and fills the channel of our blessings; we may feel these sensual scales dropping from our eyes, we may wake from this dead custom, we may be converted from this practical atheism, and inspire with a meaning we have never realized before, the familiar words of our prayer—"Give us this day our daily bread!"

III. In asking for our daily bread, we virtually ask for *ability and opportunity to obtain it.* Nor is this inconsistent with the truth upon which I have just been dwelling. For, of course, in saying that we are dependent upon God for our daily bread, I have not intended to say that it is to be acquired without the use of *means.* I have only urged the fact that God is *in* the means. And, therefore, I observe now, that, in this prayer, we ask God *for* the means, for those faculties and agencies by which our food, and all temporal necessaries are to be secured. No sane man will be apt to run into the extreme of fatalism in regard to *these* interests. As to his spiritual welfare, he may sink into an apathetic and presumptuous reliance upon the work of the Deity, and may make no effort for righteousness because he expects all the movement to come from on high. Nevertheless, he sees clearly that food, raiment, animal comforts, cannot be possessed without diligent exertion.

But the error to which I now refer, consists in the fact that we do not go *beyond* the means; that we do not sufficiently consider our dependence upon God for this strength of ours, this ability and wisdom by which we accomplish and attain. Of course, when we pray —"Give us this day our daily bread," we do not mean

—"Let it drop, like manna, from heaven—let it come to us by some new process." But, devoutly recognizing the Providence that is in every law of nature, and that really gives us these needed blessings, the essential meaning of our petition is—"Give us health, and skill, and opportunity." Devoutly acknowledging the beneficence that bursts out in the harvest, do we sufficiently recognize the wonder of the *hand* that sowed the seed, and the *thought* that planned the method? Is not this *bodily organism* molded as it is with such symmetry, woven with such manifold textures, strung with a thousand chords, a more essential gift than any material work it accomplishes? Is not *reason* a more exhaustless capacity than the hammer, the printing-press, or the steam-engine? Do we feel our dependence upon God for our daily bread, then, and not for the *life* that animates the industrious arm, and for the *thought* that underlies all human achievement? When we breathe this prayer, it is not immediately for temporal necessaries that we ask, so much as for the instruments by which these are to be acquired; thankfully owning our intimate dependence for these upon the source of all power and all thought.

And this leads us to consider the *blessedness* of these means. My friends, let us appreciate the ordinance by which it is necessary to use the means before we can obtain our daily bread, or any temporal good. Considering the benefit of strenuous thought and diligent exertion, should we not be thankful that bread does not come *spontaneously* to our hands? In one word, is not *Labor* a wise and glorious ordinance of Providence, an ordinance to be remembered in our prayers and our thanksgivings? To be sure, we can imagine a world in which there is no work. A world bathed in incessant summer, whose seed-times and harvests are ever mingling, whose springing influences perpetually ascend, whose fruitage perpetually ripens, through all the procession of its golden year. A world in which man would never feel the sting of want, and where the felicities of being would unfold without his effort. But we cannot conceive any such world, connected with human peculiarities and necessities, one half, one tithe so glorious as our old world of *struggle* and of *labor*. For, wherever God has admitted man's agency, the noblest results, the achievements of real worth and splendor, are the fruits of patient and sinewy toil. They have come from the suggestions of want and the problems of difficulty; they have been won in wrestling with the elements; they have been torn from the womb of nature. Labor, with its coarse raiment and its bare right arm, has gone forth in the earth achieving the truest conquests, and rearing the most durable monuments. It has opened the domain of matter, and the empire of mind. The wild beast has fled before it, and the wilderness has fallen back. The rock at its touch has grown plastic, and the stream obsequious. It has tilled the soil, and planted cities. Discovery accompanies it with its compass and telescope. Invention proclaims it with its Press, and heralds it through the earth with its flaming chariot. It is enriched with "the wealth of nations." It is crowned with the trophies of intellect. Its music rises in the shout of the mariner, the song of the husbandman, the hum of multitudes. It rings in the din of hammers and the roar of wheels. Its triumphal march is the progress of civilization. There are lands of luxurious climate and almost spontaneous production; yet who looks there for freedom and virtue, for the bravest hearts and the noblest souls? But the elements of liberty, the glories of intelligence, the sanctities of home, and the institutions of religion, abide in sterner soil and beneath colder skies—where the fisherman feels his way through the mist that wraps the iron sea-coast, and the reaper snatches his harvest from the skirts of winter. And who would not pray—"Give us the manly nerve, the strenuous will, and the busy thought, rather than golden *placers* and diamond mines?" And, instead of a realm sick with spontaneous plenty and desolate with riches, who would not prefer the granite fields that grudge their latent bounty, since they induce not only the exertions but the *blessings* of toil?

In asking for our daily bread, then, let us consider that, essentially, we ask for the *means* of obtaining it, and let us remember also the blessing involved in the very *effort* for acquisition.

IV. As we ask God for our daily bread, the answer to our prayer should remind us not only of our dependence upon Him, but of the relative dependence of others upon *us*. My friends; have we, after all, ever known what it is to lack bread? Have we ever lifted this cry in the bitterness of intense hunger, and in absolute want? While we have thus prayed, have we not always been surrounded with plenty, and a plenty which sometimes induces forgetfulness of God? But if this usual abundance were removed from us, perhaps, we should discover that then, for the first time, we had prayed, in sincerity, "Give us this day our daily bread." And yet, this piercing cry does go up from wasted fields and famine-smitten nations, from the lanes and cellars of cities, from homes of destitution all around us. Nor does this prayer issue merely from the lips of those who would have their daily bread without exertion, without using the *means*. A more sad and fearful utterance is the cry—"Give us *work*, that we may earn and eat and live."

Now we cannot use this prayer with any consistency, if these wants are unheeded by us, or if we merely touch them with a cold and stingy charity. The call which we make upon our heavenly Father, rebukes the central sin of *selfishness*, the spring of all other sins. The words—"Give *us*," forbid all narrow interest, all personal limitation. We are not sincere in its utterance, unless our sympathy is as responsive to others, as we would have God's help to us. We do not comprehend the obligations involved in our constant dependence upon God, unless we earnestly consider the problems of society, and act upon the idea of human-brotherhood.

V. *Finally*, for a practical purpose, I direct your attention to the proper translation of the language of the text. Its precise meaning has been differently interpreted, but it appears that the most respectable authorities render the words "*daily bread*,"—"Bread for *subsistence*,"* "*Give us bread for subsistence.*" Using the term "*bread*,"—as I have throughout this discourse—as an equivalent for all temporal provisions, I draw from this translation of these words the inference that we should be careful as to what ends we apply our earthly blessings, and for what purposes we desire them. "Bread for *subsistence*," *necessary* temporal good that is; not provisions for luxury, ostentation, or pride. Now, it is not to be supposed that a precise limit is set in this case—that no end is to be sought in desiring material

*See Maurice on the Lord's Prayer, p. 69.

good except a bare support. Wealth has its ministry. Elegance and refinement have their ministries. There would be no reservoirs of public bounty, no exhibitions of noble charity, were not suber-abundant means accumulated by some. There would be no great improvements, no large enterprises without this. The capital of a country is more to it than material riches—than so much gold and silver. It is the spring of a mighty power, it may minister to the best ends, it contains incalculable possibilities. In a rich country, we find the finest culture, the most ample elements of civilization. So, a rich man may not only gratify his own tastes, but help and improve all with whom he connects himself. In short, I would not deny that there are many arguments for wealth and refinement. And yet I maintain that the language of the text does not warrant us in asking for anything merely to gratify pride, or love of power, or love of ease. All that we are to ask for, in this, is simply *needed* material good. Let the great Disposer bestow wealth and its benefits as He will. If besides our daily bread these come to us, then how much greater our responsibilities!

But are there not many who, if they should confine their petition to this interpretation, would find their worldly desires much narrowed from their present scope? Tell me, what animates the eager toil of thousands?

What is the prayer expressed by their *action?* Is it not, evidently, a prayer for the means not merely of subsistence and comfort, not merely for refinement and benevolence, but for sensual gratification, display, and power? Is not hunger after pleasure, the epicurean lust of luxury, the vanity of ostentation, the rivaly of fashion, often, at the heart of it? Nay, is not the love of earthly good *for itself alone,* the fire that burns in the souls of many? Is not this the reason why the seeker for wealth is never satisfied? Why always he plunges among the cares of business, and never retires to rest, to think, to pray? Or if he *does* pray, is there any consistency between his prayer—"Give us this day bread *for subsistence,*" and his thirsty seeking?

While, then, we leave to God the amount of our earthly good, surely this prayer sincerely uttered can express no inordinate sensual desire; but a wise supplication and a trustful content. Says the apostle—"Ye ask, and receive not, because ye ask amiss, that ye may consume it upon your lusts." Is not this the spirit in which too many breathe even the simple prayer—"Give us this day our daily bread?"

Thus have I endeavored to exhibit the significance of the text, the manner in which we can consistently utter it, and the practical inferences that may be drawn from it. I close with two or three general remarks.

Consider, then, I beseech you, the force of this word *daily*. Is not the petition of the text one that should be daily lifted up? Are not our wants always new? Are not His mercies fresh, every morning and evening?

Again, let the language of the text suggest that deeper want to which I have alluded; that spiritual need, and that bread that cometh down from heaven.

And let me close the consideration of the text, by again referring to the beautiful lesson of Providence which it teaches. Let our hearts be impressed with the thought that He whom we ask for our daily bread, is always round about us, noticing our wants, refreshing all the springs of bounty, and holding all the issues of being; for it is a joyful and a sanctifying thought.

Especially is this truth suggested by the present season.* Standing upon the threshold of Spring, we witness, as it were, the developments of a new creation. An unseen Hand has rolled the earth through the zodiac, and prepared it for fresh and abundant life. The dark ground gives now but little promise; yet we know that, already, a marvellous process stirs in its alembics, and its veins thrill with secret inspiration. A method which we cannot comprehend, will, in due time, clothe it with vernal loveliness, and with summer wealth. Touched anew by the conviction of a Power working far outside

* This discourse was preached March 4th.

the circle of our own agency—a power which furnishes every morsel of our daily bread—we also detect, in the mechanism of things about us, the mystic intercourse of human endeavor and infinite help. In the unfolding energies of spring-time, we read not only a call to pray, but a summons to *labor*.

So let us believe in this Providence, working for us and co-operating with us, in all the mazy discipline of our lot. Let it be a cheerful thought for us in hours of sadness. Let us lean upon it in our weakness and dismay. Let us filially seek the succor it proffers and love the communion it opens. Let it fortify us with faith. Let it animate us to duty. Let us cherish it with devout humility and calm reliance. Content, obedient, let us both wait and act in the midst of this Divine hospitality, these rich incentives, and that sheltering care.

DISCOURSE VI.

"And forgive us our debts, as we forgive our debtors."—Matthew vi. 12.

The petition which we considered in the last discource, issues from the depths of our mortality, and betrays our relationship to all the forms of earthly being. For, more or less, articulately, that desire—"Give us this day our daily bread," goes up from every material thing. It rises from the dwellings of men, and the den of the wild beast; from the bird that beats the trackless air, and from the herb that waits for the summer rain. All nature looks up for its food, and we, I repeat, as members of the great whole, thus express our share in the common want.

But the petition at which we have now arrived, springs from a depth profounder than any animal necessity. It bespeaks a hunger and thirst which no material good can satisfy. It shows that the roots of man's being pierce below the mold of sense, and are involved with the mysteries of the eternal world. The cry—"Forgive us our debts, as we forgive our debtors," bursts from a *moral* being; from a being who is a *child* as well as a *creature* of God—from a being of free-will, of spiritual experience, and immortal destiny.

The text expresses both a *desire*, and its *qualification* —"Forgive us our debts" on the one hand; "as we forgive our debtors," on the other. Of itself, then, it is separated into two general divisions, under which I shall arrange the remarks I have to make at this time.

I. I observe, then, that the words which compose the first branch of the text, express *a consciousness of sin.* Whether we employ the term "*debts,*" or "*trespasses,*" we mean essentially the same thing. They are used interchangeably by Jesus. Either conveys the idea of *guilt* both in conduct and in obligation; by omission and commission. And whatever may be the direction of that guilt, whether manifested against ourselves and styled *vice,* or against our fellow-men and called *crime,* or especially against God and termed *sin*—it is all in reality, sin, for its spirit is resisted by His sanctions, and to Him we must look for absolute pardon. He is indissolubly mingled with the ideas of Right and Wrong, and no self-discipline, or restitution, will suffice unless we are reconciled to Him.

First of all, then, I say, it is a *consciousness of sin,* which breathes through these words. This is the conviction which has seized upon our souls, if the prayer is a sincere one. Otherwise, it is only form and mockery. Let me, therefore, speak more at large of this sentiment.

The ideas of Right and Wrong, are as universal as the race. God's unwritten law is known in regions where His written requirements have never penetrated. Conscience maintains its oracle in every human soul. Witnesses to this fact break out under the thickest ignorance, the most degrading sensualism, the most hideous idolatries, as well as in the confessions of the most sainted minds. Athwart all the lines of custom, beneath all forms of civilization and religion, broods an uneasy feeling of guilt, alienation, unworthiness, which whether expressed in sighs or ceremonials, whether it quivers in sacrificial flames, or murmurs—"*God be merciful unto me!*" is, essentially, the same thing. Flashing out from the personal centre of each, it reveals a yet profounder centre—the centre of a common consciousness, throbbing with a sense of sin; the axis of man's moral world, as it were, declined from its true poise and level. And this universal consciousness, more than any physical resemblance, proves the identical nature and origin of mankind. It matters but little what diversities philosophers may detect with callipers and dissecting-knife, in configuration or in color, so long as we discover the unbroken unity of this great moral deep heaving in every breast.

But consider also the *power* of this consciousness. It is true it may brood vaguely in the soul. But when it is aroused there is no element within us so mighty. There is no voice so persistent as the voice of offended conscience. There is no burden so heavy as the burden of guilt. When once a man really feels that he has done a great wrong, so long as it is unconfessed and unrepented of he cannot get rid of the feeling. The conviction sticks in him like an arrow. Nothing clings so closely to him. " When I kept silence," says the Psalmist, " my bones waxed old through my roaring." The man in whom the consciousness of guilt is awake, may journey through many lands, but he can no more travel away from the thorny fact than from himself. He may precipitate his whole nature in external activity, and forget this abiding tenant for a time ; it may be silenced for a little while by the jar of the world. But when he goes into the chambers of his being the old reality is there, and fresh yet. Though it may not unhinge his outward life, or color its facts, worse than the shirt of Nessus that pierced only to the marrow, this is an issue of inward torment, that burns along the arteries of memory and of thought. I might specify, and show, for instance, how a perjured spirit continually feels its false oath hurled back upon it from heaven ; how fraud spoils the taste of luxury, and makes ill-gotten wealth a cankering chain, how murder always hears its brother's blood crying from the ground, making the crowd more solitary than a wilderness, and the desert more populous than a city, while, sometimes that pale face hangs in the sunniest prospects by day, and that awful memory breeds a fountain of stark and ghastly dreams by night. I might show how these men, all unwhipped of *human* justice as they may be, in the heavy consciousness of sin, hear thunders more deep than the sentence of its judgment-seat, and are girt with a burning cincture more terrible than its punishment. Or admit—what in a more protracted discussion I would *not* admit—that there really can be such a thing as a conscience worn out, or slain; suppose as *apparently* is often the case, that such a man lives without trouble for his wicked deeds, heedless and happy. After all, his joy is a sickly fancy, not the spontaneous ease of spiritual health. His carelessness is a strenuous carelessness. Even if his conscience be dead as a stone —it is as heavy too. In such a case, we may believe, that there would be a consciousness of being unconscious —a sense of life in death.

But, while I have thus endeavored to illustrate the power there is in a keen consciousness of guilt, and while, as a universal feeling, this consciousness must in some degree exist in *us*, how comes it, as is often the case, that it is not distinct and strong? Do we say "because we are not thus grossly guilty?" Do we slumber upon the fact of ordinary good conduct, of respectable conformity, and negative innocence. If this is our feeling, we can never earnestly breathe the words —"Forgive us our debts." Perhaps a slight sense of general unworthiness may animate this petition, when we employ it at all; or it may burst from our lips upon the fresh consciousness of some wrong overt act; and yet we do not feel the vitality of the sentiment expressed in the prayer. Let us remember that an undisturbed conscience is no proof of innocence. This may result from spiritual indolence and carelessness; from lack of self-examination. A man may do wrong every day, and yet feel no compunction for that wrong, not because he has no means of knowing better, but because he never uses those means. He never looks into his own soul. He never compares it with the standard which he knows he ought to consult. He never holds it up to the mirror of truth, nor concentrates upon it the focal light of God's requirements. He lives to-day as he did yesterday, he will live in the same way to-morrow; pursuing one beaten round of habit, and, perhaps, never thinking of conscience except in some hasty snatch of thought, or when he stumbles into some transgression palpable to the most secular eyes. His conscience is undisturbed, simply because he has never disturbed it. He has this vague sense of moral unworthiness, as I have said, but he has never gone down into its depths, he has never cleft it open and let God's light in upon it, in order that he might know the *degree* of his unworthiness. It is surprising how much *habit* has to do with what is called "a quiet conscience." We can realize this sometimes, when, passing from one set of customs to another—from one circle where a morality equally conventional, yet higher in degree exists, to another where a yet lower ideal prevails. We see men whose disposition is as excellent, whose love of morality in the abstract is as quick and reverent as our own, yet who do and say things, as matters of course, that strike us with wonder and horror. This is simply the effect of custom. The conscience of these men is encrusted by habit.

Men are content too, to live as well as their neighbors, to conform to the conventional pattern of respectability, to limit their aspirations to the code of generally recognized virtues. Therefore, morality, goodness, religion, instead of being an absolute sanction, an exhaustless life, an infinite attainment, becomes a *fashion.* Each country has one of its own, and its well-meaning citizens would not like to fall below it, and do not strive much to going beyond it. If one does fall below it, he sinks into social disrepute. If he does run beyond it, he risks being called a fanatic.

There is a morality of *trade*, and, if one conforms to that, he and his conscience agree very well. He eats heartily and sleeps peacefully, without thought of bringing his conscience into the light of prayerful introspection, and of comparing it with the *christian* code. Or, if this thought has sometimes occurred to him, he has put by its suggestion as something disagreeable and impracticable, and relapsed into the consolatory maxim, that he is as good as his neighbors. There is a morality of *politics*—a very plastic morality it is too—yet respectable men, without any qualms of conscience, will adopt it in an election campaign, while they would not employ it in the ordinary routine of life; and they actually seem to think that there *is* a sense in which the policy of party may over-ride the ordinances of God. There is a morality of *social life*, very bland and courteous, nay, sometimes *exceedingly* virtuous; and yet though it often lacks heart, and is decorated with a lie, those who maintain it make no complaints of conscience.

Thus, we perceive that an unconsciousness of sin may ensue from a lack of personal examination; from a monotonous and conventional ideal, beyond whose limits men do not look or aspire. Nay, it must be confessed that *systems of theology* may sometimes induce this comparative unconsciousness. While in one set of tenets God and man have been presented in a manner altogether too stern and gloomy, it may be the tendency of another class to put too much out of sight the evil of sin, so that, even in our devotions, while we are thankful and prayerful, we but too little feel the malignity of guilt and the keenness of remorse, and we may be unconscious that this guilt is magnified by the very light in which we regard the character of God. Thus absorbed in contemplation of what the Deity will do, we may lose sight of what we ought to do; we may not sufficiently explore our own hearts and contrast our inner life with the ideal presented by Christ.

But, whatever may be the cause of our unconsciousness of sin, the main point is that that unconsciousness is no evidence of the absence of sin. If a man will solicitously ask himself how he lives—from what motives and to what ends—if he compares himself as he is with what he knows he should be; if he will do this humbly and prayerfully, he will find ample need for the petition now before us. Nay, he may find that his very unconsciousness of sin is itself a great sin, a sign of moral apathy that should not exist amid the sanctions and claims that press upon him. He may find that he has as much cause, or more, for a pungent sense of guilt, as even the perjured or fraudulent man to whom I alluded; and he may detect a keen personal application in the words of our Savior—" Those eighteen upon whom the tower in Siloam fell, and slew them, think ye that they were sinners above all men that dwelt in Jerusalem?"

Let any one seriously examine himself, let him consider candidly his sins of *thought, word,* and *deed,* nay, let him count up the number of these even in the course of a single day, and, surely, a strong consciousness of evil will spring up fresh within him. But let us not confine ourselves to *positive* faults. Let us not merely consider our *trespasses*—our sins of *com*mission; but our *debts,* our sins of *o*mission; and this consciousness will become more stringent. First of all, let us consider our great obligations to God, consider what He is, consider His goodness towards us and how we have repaid it—the legion of temporal mercies that encompass us, the spiritual blessings culminating in the cross of Christ; our un-performed duties, our unimproved opportunities, the capacities of a single day compared with the use which we have made of it; let us, after all this, unlock our own hearts, enter into their subtle windings, and challenge the motives that lurk in their secret chambers, and this prayer would burst from our lips as never before.

Let us, in the next place, endeavor to discover the *meaning* of this petition—"Forgive us our debts." Uttered as it is, or should be, with a vivid consciousness, what do we desire and expect to be done for us? I answer, that our essential wish, mingled with poignant regret, is to be reconciled to God—to feel that He has, as it were, forgotten our transgressions, and turns upon us the light of His countenance. The belief that our sins are forgiven causes us to possess a full sense of rest; the troubled mind grows calm, its tormenting suggestions sink as the waves sunk when Christ said, "Peace be still." This is the *subjective* method of forgiveness, vaguely expressed, as all spiritual experiences must be; this is our own feeling as to pardon—and I do not know that it is necessary for our philosophy to penetrate further. It does not alter the substantial result to know precisely what is *meant* by the forgiveness of sin; whether it simply implies reconciliation, or whether the punishment of sin is remitted also. Whether, although there is the peace of repentance there must still ensue the intrinsic retribution of the guilty act. The original word, which is here translated *"forgive,"* may be rendered *"remit," "send away,"* and the main idea of the petition seems to be—"remove this heavy incumbrance of guilt, this painful indebtedness of evil." Even if, after this the natural consequence of sin ensues, is it not an evidence of God's goodness, of His fixed and wise discipline?

But, in speaking of punishment, let us distinguish between its intrinsic sting and its more external peculiarities. Let us not reduce it to the equivalent of a mere physical law, which cannot be suspended. The intrinsic evil of all sin is *moral,* and its profoundest retribution is *moral* also. The sense of alienation, the spiritual deadness, the remorse, the inner wo, these are as judicial sentences, and penal fires. And when that guilt is removed, when that alienation gives place to reconciliation, when that spiritual deadness is exchanged for newness of life, when that remorse turns to gratitude and that inner wo to peace, is not the retribution dismissed with the sin in which it was involved? Is not the punishment inevitably forgiven with the guilt? Consider, too, how much suffering there is in repentance itself; how much agony, bitterness, and shame. Is not this a part of retribution? We may believe then that the vital element of retribution is dismissed with the sin; and, indeed, when we have got so far as heartily to cry—"Forgive us our debts," retribution has accomplished at least one of its great purposes. Again, I say, that this sense of pardon and retribution appears to be the practical one, whatever our philosophy may determine. It is enough for the truly penitent soul; it was enough for weeping Mary, and denying Peter; it is enough for any who come, and sincerely cry—"Forgive us our debts."

But, once more, I observe that the best evidence of our sincerity in this prayer, will be our *corresponding conduct.* It affords a peculiar illustration of the fact that true prayer blends desire with action. Certainly we do not truly repent of the sin which we easily resume, and habitually cherish. It is not really forgiven —*remitted, sent away.* It was merely repudiated by a gush of feeling; denounced only by the lips. At least, the sin we pray against we must struggle against, and by God's help overcome. Oh! it is solemn mockery to ask pardon for the sin we love and mean to retain—to go deliberately and *do* the very thing we have prayed we might do no more, or to withhold our hand from that which we have prayed we might perform. The evidence that this prayer is sincere, will be seen either in *abstinence* or *performance,* in *restitution* or in *example.* He who utters it, will abandon his old habit of wrong. His lips and his hands will be restrained. His heart will be guarded, and his thoughts disciplined. Or, he will run in paths that he has too much neglected; he will show new love, new zeal, new forms of action. Nay, there will be no more striking evidence of his sincerity, than the fact that the power with which he has committed trespasses, will be poured into new channels for discharging obligations. Or the wrong that such an one has done to a fellow-man, will be repaired if possible. And yet how many evils are there, even in regard to our fellow-men, that cannot be repaired. What grievous injury have we often committed, for instance, in our *example*. Not only have we furnished them with no incentive to truth and goodness by our walk and conversation, but perhaps our influence has been exerted upon them for positively bad ends; even though we may not have intended that influence. And there can hardly be a keener subject of remorse than this fact, when we call it up in retrospect. For this injury we can make no restitution except by lives of virtue and religion in the future.

In these, or in other forms, then, we shall show the sincerity of our prayer. I shall not be understood to say, in any sense, that we can repay God for the wrong we have done. Notwithstanding all we may do for ourselves and others, our indebtedness to Him remains. But I have merely urged the fact that corresponding action is a necessary adjunct to our verbal petition. That without it there is no true desire, no real forgiveness, however earnestly we may say—"Forgive us our debts."

II. The last remark naturally introduces us to the second division of the text—"As we forgive *our debtors*." Here is suggested at once a general course of *action*, without which the prayer—"Forgive us our debts," is nugatory. There is a qualification, or condition to our desire, without which that desire has no efficacy or reality. It is a condition upon which our Savior emphatically insists. He returns to it immediately after the close of the prayer, and says—"For if ye forgive men their trespasses, your heavenly Father will also forgive you: but, if ye forgive not men their trespasses, neither will your heavenly Father forgive your trespasses." Again, in Mark, he says—"When ye stand praying, *forgive*, if ye have ought against any: that your Father which is in heaven may forgive you your trespasses. But if ye do not forgive, neither will your Father which is in heaven forgive your trespasses." And most strikingly has he illustrated the same doctrine in the parable of the two Debtors.

Now that there are some limitations to these, as to all general statements, will not be denied. We do not suppose that the forgiveness of others is the *sole* condition of onr pardon, whether we perform other duties or not. Nor need we understand it as forbidding us to claim our just dues, nor even as condemning the infliction of punishment, for, as we have seen, the spirit of forgiveness may co-exist with the exercise of punishment. We cannot suppose that the doctrine of the text means anything that would really impair the moral law, or unhinge society; but it is certain that this requirement to forgive others, is no *light* requirement—no *secondary* principle. It must not be narrowed or weakened; it must not be thrust aside for an ordinary exception; it must not be sophistically explained away by our interest, or our passion; it must not be neglected as an impracticable abstraction. It is a vital condition that Christ thus imposes upon us, and, ere we give it utterance, ere we weld it into our burning desire for pardon before the mercy-seat, it will be well for us to consider its meaning, and the heed we give to it.

One fact seems clear—that if we consistently utter the words in the text, we cannot harbor before God a grudge towards any man. There is no wound so deep that we may cherish malice towards him who inflicted it. There is no quarrel so serious that we can exclude our antagonist from our pardoning sentiment. There is no posture of affairs between ourselves and another that will justify our setting him aside as a just exception. If there might only be that *one* exception, perhaps we could utter this conditional petition freely. We could look about us then and say—"We are at peace with all." But this particular case must not be brought into the question. "Excuse that. Do not touch it. It is a sore point. Do not insist against *that* hardness; surely the condition was never meant to reach so far as that." And yet, *that* is the very thing that balks the whole petition. *That* is the very point which Christ touched so emphatically; and until that particular obstacle melts away, this prayer—

"Forgive us our debts, as we forgive our debtors," is a mockery. "Forgive us our debts, as we forgive those against whom we entertain no grudge!" Why, what would be the significance of *such* a prayer? But for the very reason that it *is* a hard point to surrender our cherished enmity; for the very reason that it costs a pang and a mighty struggle, to pluck out pride from our hearts, and to extract our rankling revenge; the condition is so keenly pressed upon us. And yet, when I think how often this prayer may be breathed while this reservation is really made; when I think too, how common is the lust of revenge, how hastily it is adopted, how intimately it becomes entangled with our pride, our prejudice, and our interest; how sad and wide-spread, often, is its operation; how it breaks up the fellowship of men, transmutes bosom-friends to foes, divides families, and causes persecution, ruin, and murder; how it lies as a bitter ingredient in so many cups, and bites like a secret viper in so many hearts; and yet these words —"Forgive us our debts," such solemn, such profound words, are so frequently mingled with the qualification —"as we forgive our debtors, "I cannot but wonder at the formality and insignificance of our devotion. For, I repeat, these are no *light* words. This is no unimportant doctrine that shines so among the leaves of the New Testament. When we lift up our hearts to the all-

all-seeing God, we must embrace in the circle of our thought, all who have trespassed against us—all who are morally indebted to us—and as, in our clinging weakness, our remorse, and our shame, we cry to Him for pardon, so must we pardon them!

And, of course, that which must thus break as a devout sentiment from our hearts, and direct our hands, must appear in our conduct. If there is one feeling in the bosom of man that is full and strong like the ocean-tide, it is the feeling that promptly rises to revenge an injury. If there is one memory that burns in the soul like an everlasting flame, it is the memory of a wrong. Old grudges are locked in the heart for years, and bequeathed as heir-looms. An insult is repaid with interest. A refusal to accommodate at one time is emphatically compensated by a counter-refusal. Or if we have been able somewhat to overcome this madness of retaliation; if we refuse to give back wrong for wrong; how much harder is it to overcome the reluctance to *benefit* those who have injured us—to pardon and to bless them? Or, if we have reached even this degree of Christian temper, have we not performed the good act remembering that such deeds heap coals of fire upon the heads of our enemies—and have we not been sadly disappointed if the coals did not *scorch?* But not even this degree of forgiveness is attained by the many. Generally, the irritation is nursed and kept raw; and with what a thrill of pleasure does the abused clutch the abuser, exclaiming—"It is *my* turn now!" And if, in the name of Christ, we bid that uplifted hand forbear, and that surcharged spirit of revenge distill in pardon, are we not regarded as fanatical? Are we not told that we are preaching an impracticable virtue—that we are endeavoring to thwart human nature with abstractions? Doubtless, such a spirit *is* contrary to the customary practices and the darling ideals of men; but we are learning now of a higher oracle than this world. To you O man! whoever you are, if you are conscious that you need pardon, that you are weak, tempted, guilty; if you would cry to the merciful God—"Forgive us our debts;" to *you* is proclaimed the inevitable condition—"as we forgive our debtors." And do you say that this is an impossible condition? Nay it has been *lived*, and in the same *spirit* may be lived again. See —scourged, mocked, spit upon, *who*, with meek face, lifts up that bloody brow and breathes a prayer of pardon? Reviled, he reviles not again. Suffering, he threatens not. Oppressed, afflicted, "as a lamb brought to the slaughter, as a sheep before her shearers is dumb, so he openeth not his mouth." *Who* is this? He who bids us forgive as we would be forgiven; and who, in the judgment-hall, and on the cross, exhibited his precepts in action. I know that the standard of the world is below this, and the heart of man chafes at it, but if we would render allegiance to *his* teachings, this is the spirit that must control us.

And now, perhaps, we can see why Christ laid such stress upon this particular virtue of Forgiveness. He urged it thus strongly, because it is a virtue so difficult to practice, because it costs so much effort and sacrifice. For before we can truly accomplish it, we must surrender some of the deepest feelings in our breasts. We must give up not only hate, but pride and self-will. Our obstinate hearts must be penetrated and melted by the spirit of Christian Love. After all, as a general thing, our spirit of revenge does not long retain its fierce edge, it is not always a hot and wild passion, but subsides into a more quiet resentment. Still it is nourished by our jealousy, by the conceit of dignity, and by the desire for consistency. We wish to show our enemy and the world that we are enough for him; that we have persistency and toughness; that we can give back blow for blow, scorn for insult. *We* will not be the first to hang out a flag of truce, or to make advances! But let him change his antagonistic abuse and our crested pride will be apt to droop, our alarmed sensitiveness to subside. I cannot believe that, commonly, a man's heart is so hard that he will not pity a fallen enemy, and quench his vindictiveness at the sight of his misfortunes. When our old foe stands helpless, what is there for us to oppose and injure? And when he sleeps his last sleep, when he lies before us still and nerveless, when we gaze once for all upon that face which we have remembered to hate, and think how cold that heart is which hated us, death looks so rebukingly to us that it melts all our stubbornness and wrings our spirits with regret. We would not, if we could, follow him with our revenge. We would not plant it upon the grassy mound, nor intrude it into the sacred privacy of the grave. Passion, perhaps, has been spent long ago, but it required something like this before our *pride* would yield. But the requirement is, that before this necessary crisis we should give up that pride. If the true spirit of the prayer had influenced us at an earlier period, how much bitterness might have been spared to us, and to him who now lies yonder! With what different feelings might we have cherished his memory!

But not only does the condition in the text require a difficult, but a profound work on our part, for it demands the renunciation of *selfishness.* And, after all, this is the essential evil which it opposes. This is at the bottom of all our revenge. This keeps green the roots of our enmity. This is expressed in that hateful wilfulness which nerves us to maintain our own rights at all cost, to press them to the last limit—even to the pound of flesh. When we speak of our "*debtors*," we refer not merely to our enemies, but to all who by any chance in life depend upon our mercy, or need our consideration. If we really forgive, then we promise not to be hard with them, not to insist upon every exaction, not to claim with unfeeling tenacity all things accidentally due to our position; but to exercise a self-sacrificing amenity. How deeply, then, into our customs and dispositions, does this condition cleave! It calls, I repeat, for nothing less than the eradication of selfishness; it implies nothing less than the ingathering of the full spirit of Christ's Love. We are so situated in this life that as we are dependent upon others, so thousands are dependent upon us, indebted to us for our word or our deed, our mercy and our aid; and we are called upon to cherish the disposition of that God to whom we pray. How awful would be the truth, were He nothing but infinite Self-Will—a self-will using power without regard to the welfare of His creatures. And how glorious is the fact that He is infinite Love, ever seeking our benefit! And yet, is not self-will the ruling principle in the world? Is it not the festering plague and the desolating force, that afflicts and overthrows? And when we reflect upon the change that this spirit of forgiveness would induce, do we wonder that Christ urged it so impressively? Do we wonder that he made it a great condition in our pardon? Nay, is it not an *essential* condition? For, how can we be forgiven unless we do forgive? How can we have our sin remitted, sent away, unless hatred, revenge, selfishness the root of all sin, be removed from us? Is not the one by the inevitable nature of things, the measure of the other?

In various relations of life, then, does the qualification in the prayer apply to man. It applies to you, oh hard-hearted exactor, grinding the faces of the poor; to you oh unmerciful one, urging your private malignity in the name of justice; to you, oppressor, peeling the flesh of men with the iron and the scourge—to all of us, who in any relation of life, restrain the spirit of christian kindness and forbearance.

My friends, if this petition were sincerely uttered in christian closets and christian churches, society would be leavened with a new life, and molded into a far better shape. Mighty has been the antagonism in the world between Christ's spirit of *mercy* and man's spirit of *selfishness*. Where the one has gone abroad as an iron force, the other has proceeded as a moral power. Where the one has swept like the tempest, the other has followed like the summer dawn. Where the one has embattled armed legions, the other has sent Teachers of truth, Missionaries of peace, and Sisters of Charity. Where the one has bleached the earth with human bones, the other has clothed it with shining harvests. Where the one has reared shambles of lust and marts of mammon, the other has built asylums and hospitals and opened countless channels of benevolence. Where the one has blotted heaven with the smoke of worldliness and shut us in with walls of materialism, the other has revealed the starry prospect of immortality. Where the one has degraded man, nourished skepticism and engendered despair, the other has kindled in the soul a consciousness of its destiny, and poured the great influences of redemption.

This struggle is still going on. Even now does the spirit of Christ's mercy question the selfishness of those codes, by which in the name of punishment man gratifies revenge, and for the sake of *preservation* insists upon *destruction.* The ample Christianity of the Gospels gathers even the tainted criminal into its fold, and while it bids us *protect* also bids us *spare.* While it sanctions retribution it urges us to see to it that retribution itself becomes a healing chastisement. Even now do we discover the wisdom of saving rather than destroying, and learn that a renewed soul is a better guarantee for society than a hateful victim; that no community is so safe as that where God's attributes are sovereign in their essential unity—a community strong with that Justice which is the pillar, that Mercy which is the glory of His Throne.

Still wider than we can prophecy, more deep than we can fathom, this spirit of mercy will contend with this spirit of selfishness. But who can doubt the issue? Who that has ever felt the need, or extended the blessing of forgiveness?

DISCOURSE VII.

"And lead us not into temptation."—Matthew vi: 13.

THE prayer for the pardon of sin is coupled with a sense of *spiritual weakness.* The moral condition that excites desire for the one, suggests the liabilities of the other. In the retirement of devotion, the world falls away from us, its busy machinery stops, and its complex shapes of *action* are arranged in the order of *contemplation.* Then, a man may look calmly back upon his past conduct and explore the windings of his own heart. He may wonder at the slight causes that have driven him astray; at the phantoms he has followed and embraced; at the poverty of the draught which has intoxicated, at the baseness of the chains which have bound him. He may wonder that his whole soul has been so intensely mixed with perishable elements and delusive forms. For, then he is far above the chafing current of life. He sees with a clearer vision. He applies the touchstone of eternal reality.

But when, smitten with repentance, he cries for forgiveness, in that very petition, I repeat, he confesses his liability. The depth of his remorse indicates the degree of his exposure. The fact that these temporalities, worthless as they may be, have so strongly controlled him, betrays his feebleness. And into that world that now beats against his retirement, he must soon re-enter. Its bounding pulses will become mated with his own, and its hot life will settle in his veins. And, however much that world has dwindled beneath the eye of contemplation, it will expand to its old dimensions in the contact of action. The future will cast itself in the mold of the past. The bad suggestions and the fair deceits, the multitudinous hosts of evil, that seemed like dreams, stand up again awaiting him as hard realities. The ghosts of retrospect embody themselves anew, and those unsubstantial shadows as they seemed in the light of evening reflection and of morning thought, he will find to be terrible facts in the wrestlings of passion and the heat of noon-day. If he could always experience the freshness and freedom of that repentant hour; if that calm, cool Presence of God could be his tent in the busy market and the crowded street, he might venture forth with stronger confidence. But a snare may spring upon him in the very first step from the threshold. The first path he turns into may be a path of disobedience and neglect.

Besides, were the world limited to the walls of his own chamber, to the bed of sickness, to the closet of study, to the cloisters of a monastic retirement, nay, to the heart alone, and that heart in its devoutest action; how thick, even here, the forms of evil! How busy, how real; how mighty! He, then, who really *feels* his sins—who understands the atmosphere in which they thrive, the moral condition from which they spring, will instantly blend the petition now before us with that just preceding. No sooner will he say—"Forgive us our debts!" than he will pray—"Lead us not into temptation."

It will be well for us, then, to consider the *meaning* and the *applications* of this prayer, which is so necessary and so urgent.

I. I observe that this is not a prayer *against* temptation—that is, against the *circumstances* of temptation. For, this would be a prayer against all our powers and opportunities. It would be a virtual rejection of our highest nature and of our noblest privileges. If a man should ask that he might never be liable to bodily pain, it would be, essentially, a petition that he might never experience bodily pleasure; for his prayer could be answered only by the extirpation of those nerves which alike convey both sensations. If one should ask that his capability of seeing evil might be quenched, he would really ask for the destruction of his eyes; for the faculty of beholding the evil as well as the good, is the very faculty of vision itself. Following out the analogy, I would say that to pray that we never may be tempted, would be to pray that the circumstances of our present existence may have no moral significance for us. It would be a prayer that we may have no self-consciousness, and no spiritual freedom. For, if we have self-consciousness, that is, if we know the character of our conduct and our motives, this faculty must be accompanied by the power of self-direction. Why should we know the inner springs of our moral nature, their different motives and tendencies and the character of their work, unless we have this self-control? And, if we have this ability, or, in other words, this moral freedom, of course we have the power of *choice.* But, again, there is no employment for this power of choice—we could never exercise it—unless things have a diverse moral significance, unless we are solicited by the evil as well as by the good. The self-same consciousness that feels the suggestions of the one, feels the suggestions of the other. The ability to do right is the ability to do wrong. To pray, therefore, that we may not be liable to temptation, is to pray that we may never know or feel moral excellence—that we may put out the eye, and paralyze the nerves of the soul. Remove this liability, and you destroy the moral power of our nature; you obliterate the highest peculiarity of manhood. You would make man as a brute—nay, as a planet, driven and attracted upon the plane of an inevitable orbit.

But more than this, temptation is the instrument of all self-productive power—of all spontaneous moral energy. It is the test of all virtue ; nor can we conceive the attainment of virtue, without its existence and opposing action. Virtue is not innocence, or mere abstinence from guilt. It is positive excellence. It is an acquired skill. It is tne allegiance of free-will, and the consummate grace of a disciplined nature. It does not unfold itself as an intrinsic sentiment, it does not come by an easy acquiescence in things ; but it is, with God's help, *gained*, as the intellect acquires its power and the right hand its cunning, by resisting and overcoming obstacles.

Now, we may puzzle ourselves with presumptuous speculations. We may curiously ask whether God could not have made man holy and happy without this tremendous exposure—without going through these battles of temptation ? It will not do for us to dogmatize in this elevated region of inquiry. But, speaking earnestly, I will say, that I cannot conceive how God could have made man a creature of progress, a being of vital and original morality, without bestowing upon him this contingent power, and throwing him in contact with evil. I cannot conceive man's attaining the ideal of holiness and happiness which now lies within his reach, without the self-same condition in which he now exists. "But," says a shrewd philosopny, "God made man's circumstances and man's nature; to whom, then, is the blame of sin to be referred? Is man guilty if he yields, his nature being so weak and temptation so strong?" But suppose we answer this by assuming another philosophy. Admitting that God ordained the circumstances and created the nature of man, it does not follow that he made the *evil* of the one or the *weakness* of the other. But this may exist as an intrinsic necessity in things, which could not be prevented any more than the finite could be made infinite.. But suppose, while this exists as a necessary condition, we behold God pouring out all positive excellence, ordaining all order, harmony, beauty, virtue; ever working against evil and calling upon man, His moral image, everywhere to do the same, to be his co-worker; and suppose man neglects this Divine solicitation, refuses this Divine help, suffers his spiritual energies to weaken and to waste, and therefore of his own will resists not but yields to sin; where then does the blame fall? Suppose too, that even foreseeing man would often fall, God foresaw the most glorious result of the whole, and thus, as the best election among many possibilities, ordained the present scheme, can we in aught object?

I do not present the above as an established theory of

sound as the notion that Omnipotence means the power of accomplishing inconsistencies as well as possibilities; that God made essential evil as well as good; that the murder committed by Cain was really as acceptable to Him as the sacrifice offered by Abel; and that, though summoning man to resist sin and making the richest provisions for his escape from it, in doing that sin he is accomplishing His will as much as in overcoming it or flying from it. I do not expect to strain every moral problem through the alembic of reason; but, if one of these two theories *must* be selected, I prefer the one which I have just suggested.

But, my friends, there is no need of metaphysical theories upon the subject now before us. For, whatever philosophy we adopt, the blame is not in the fact of being tempted, but of *yielding* to temptation. Our nature may be feeble, and our circumstances may teem with evil suggestions, but we are not obliged to surrender. No necessity drives us to sin. We are encouraged by God and by every good thing to resist and to stand fast, we are furnished with divine help, and our highest achievement, is, by that help, in overcoming evil. And when we fall, we fall voluntarily. Says the poet—

> "Evil into the mind of God or man
> May come and go, so *unapproved*, and leave
> No spot or blame behind."

And, from better authority, we know that he who came to redeem man from evil, "was tempted in all points as we are, but *without sin.*" The solicitous wrong leaves no taint in our souls if we let it pass by, but the *cherishing* it, and *yielding* to it, is the sin. And when we do this, we do it freely. We do it knowing that it is wrong, and that we have power to do otherwise. Ours, and ours alone, therefore, is the blame.

Such, then, are the nature and the consequences of temptation. And if our weakness, our shame, our guilt are involved with it, so are our freedom, our power, our holiness and our happiness. Therefore, we cannot pray that we may not be liable to temptation, or that we may not be tempted. We cannot shrink in moral cowardice from the battle before us. We cannot meanly hide our talent in the earth. We must not seek out temptation. We must not rush into it. Nay, we should avoid it. But we must not decline it; we cannot escape from it. Let us, then, with trust and with prayer press on. Let us remember that man is not a machine driven along the grooves of fixed fate, but an incalculable power sent into the universe to develop itself—a living personality precipitated upon the axis of free-will, and from its own inner impulse describing the parabola of good or evil. He is not, like material nature, the inert receptacle of a higher force and moved from without;

but, so far as the finite can resemble the Infinite he is like God, capable of original power, and, if holy, holy not by arbitrary conformity but as an essential expression of his own being. Nor is there anything more solemn than the responsibility which is involved in this moral freedom; nothing more momentous than the encounter of the soul with temptation; nothing more fearful than the issues of defeat; nothing more glorious than the results of victory. But it is a responsibility of which we cannot rid ourselves. Our noblest privilege is that responsibility—our highest dignity is this power of choice.

II. But still we must assiduously lift up this prayer—"*Lead us not into temptation;* and we shall breathe it more earnestly the more we perceive the truths I have just urged. With no presumptuous confidence, but with humility and a sense of weakness, shall we go forth into the world, or treat with our own hearts. As the *second* general point in this discourse, then, let me endeavor to present the true meaning of the text. The meaning opens to us in the different though proper rendering of a single word. Instead of "*Lead* us not into temptation," it would be better to read—"Abandon us not to temptation;" which translation is sustained by good authority, as well as by the nature of things. The spirit of this prayer, then, is not directed against the circumstances of temptation, but against its *power* and in behalf of our weakness. "*Abandon* us not to temptation! We are in a world of evil suggestions. Leave us not *alone*, O God, to meet it; give us ever thy divine help and guidance; let us not go among its hosts unsheltered. Lead us not *into* temptation—let us not be ensnared by it; but lead us safely, and victoriously *through* it!"

There are various ways in which this meaning of the prayer may be specified. But perhaps we shall best express its essential significance when we say—"Suffer us not to forget *that* God is, and *what* God is." Let us not, like Peter, fall into a presumptuous confidence in our own virtue. Let us not go abroad in the world, supposing that we alone are strong enough to grapple with evil promptings and enticements. Let us remember that we need a constant sense of God's presence, a clear perception of His character, and a profound faith in His Providential succor. It has been said by another, that those who are tempted "are tempted to doubt that God is, and that He is the author of good, and not of evil; and that He is mightier than the evil; and that He can and will overthrow it, and deliver the universe out of it. This is the real temptation, there is no other."* And is it not true that men, when they yield to temptation, really forget God—is not this the radical mischief? Con-

* Maurice.

sider, for a moment. Do you suppose, if, at the time when sin is pressing you hard and when your will is about to consent, a vivid sense of God could break upon you; if a mighty consciousness of His Presence could seize upon you, and you could realize that His eye was piercing to the core of your heart; if, moreover, you had a clear perception of His moral excellence, of the supremacy of goodness as manifested in Him, and, by contrast, of the odiousness of evil, do you suppose *then* you could give way to that temptation? And is not all evil triumphant over man's will and his heart, because that strong consciousness is absent? Were it otherwise, could the murderer accomplish his bloody intent? Before he could brace himself to that horrid purpose, he must struggle with temptation; he has felt the pressure of good as well as the desire for evil. One by one, more or less reluctantly, with more or less force, he has smothered the suggestions of God in his soul. He has in *himself* put out the light, before in any other sense he could say—"Put out the light." What then, as he creeps to his deed under the canopy of darkness, what then if a sense of the instant Deity should flash upon that benumbed conscience, those drugged remonstrances in his soul? Would they not wake with irresistible energy? What if, in that lonely star that breaks through the rifted cloud, he should detect the eye of Omniscience? What if, in the passing wind, God should talk to him? What if the loveliness of the infinite Father, the glory of His moral nature, the supreme excellence of goodness, should kindle upon the horizon before him? Would evil have any power over him, then? Could any solicitation then attract him to the commission of that crime? Or, suppose that an opportunity occurs for a man to commit a profitable *fraud.* Suppose that every circumstance sharpens the evil suggestion, and spares him even the effort of invention. No human skill can detect his secret, or suspect his plan. The moral sense remonstrates for a time, but at length the biassed will conspires with the occasion. Everything is ready and urgent. What then if only the truth of God should shoot like a sunbeam through his wicked purposes? What then if he should be vividly struck with the conviction that God is, and should realize the great sanctions involved in that fact? The temptation would lose its charm, and the web of deceit drop from his trembling hands. Or take any man who lives a life of mere convenience and policy, who recognizes no higher standard than self-interest, and who values nothing but sensual good and is completely controlled by his appetites and lusts; and is not the essential error of such a life the lack of hearty belief in God? Yes, temptation is fed by practical atheism; by a vital skepticism as to moral goodness. The great truths of God and duty are dim and feeble in the soul, and covered with sensual accretions. Our action is outward and habitual rather than introspective and sincere. We live in conventionalisms, and our conventionalisms are dead at the root. Our plans, our motives, our ideals, are mixed with a confused and jarring worldliness. We test them with earthly weights and measures. We do not single them out in prayer. We do not let the light of infinite reality stream in upon them. We do not stand face to face with God. If we did, we would never practically deny the might and the worth of goodness. We never would surrender to evil. We never would be overswept by strong delusion to believe a lie; to submit to the fatal deceit that there is any real gain in sin, or any loss in virtue. Nor would we ever, in moments of intellectual perplexity, lose our faith, or, in seasons of sorrow and gloom, give place to distrust. Temptation, then, would have no edge. Our faith would prevent our deliberate yielding to sin, and would guard us from passionate surprise. Before our true ideal, the wrong, however attractive its semblance, would change and fall like Dagon.

There have lived those whose history far transcends the ordinary standard, and who are distinguished even among the great men of the earth. They strike us by their calm grandeur—by their moral force. Though dead, they are springs of an ever-fresh vitality, and their influence beats as a constant inspiration through the arteries of the race. Their dying words, though mocked at, were living prophecies, and their eyes, though they looked through veils of flame, looked far into the future. These were the heroes of the truth, the martyrs for righteousness' sake, the men who could find no compromise between right and wrong, the men who

> "——— Gave glorious chase
> To persecutions; and against the face
> Of Death and fiercest dangers, durst with brave
> And sober pace march on to meet a grave."

Sometimes they appear in a more gentle mold, and die in a less celebrated theatre. But they are all distinguished by a reliance upon something deeper than time or sense; by a stedfast rejection of evil however splendid, even though it involves the boon of life itself; by an open confession of truth even in blood and flame. Their real strength and recompense was belief in God, in the worth and the power of goodness. And that faith dwelling now in the heart of the feeblest man, shall make him stronger than all this world. In the allurements of wealth and pleasure, it shall be a safeguard and a guide. In misfortune it shall confirm religious trust, and make the bed of poverty like Jacob's stony pillow; it shall arm the heart with sublime courage and banish all the clouds of doubt. It and it alone is the strength of the tempted spirit, whatever the form of temptation.

Thus we perceive the force of the prayer—"*Abandon* us not to temptation." It is essentially an expression of faith in God. It is a Prayer that we may always entertain a sense of His presence and of His nature; and that we may not fall into practical atheism. When we sincerely breathe this petition, we are armed against sin. When we thus virtually say, we will worship the Lord our God, and Him only will we serve, the devil leaveth us. When evil solicitation presses us, and we lean upon our Father, and cry, "Abandon us not to temptation," we have an answer and a help in the prayer itself.

III. Let us consider, finally, some *circumstances* in which the prayer of the text is applicable. As a general remark, then, it is only necessary to say that the occasions of temptation are continual and multiform. They open upon us everywhere; and this petition, therefore, should always rise from our hearts But two or three special truths are suggested by this fact upon which I would dwell, in closing.

First, then I observe, that temptation, of course, will always assail our weak point. Temptation cannot exist without the concurrence of *inclination* and *opportunity*. If we are ever so much inclined to do evil and have not the *means*, we are not tempted. If we are surrounded with facilities and have not the *will* we are not tempted. No doubt a great deal that is called virtue is of this negative sort. Men are innocent of particular sins because they are not attracted to those sins. But do they resist those to which they are attracted? Are they loyal to righteousness when both desire and occasion conspire against it? *This* is the test of virtue. A man may spurn evil suggestions ninety-nine times, and yield upon the hundredth, because that jumps exactly with his inclination. And that is the point where he will begin to parley with conscience, to hunt up compromises, to invent sophistical excuses. He will endeavor to make out that the evil is not evil—or that the circumstances which now beset him are different from those that have entangled other men—or that the end is good though the means are a little oblique. All shows that now he is really tempted. All this calls upon him to pray—"*Abandon* us not to temptation." Of course, the struggle which rent the soul of the premeditating murderer would never trouble *him;* because he had no disposition to murder. He might dismiss the suggestion of fraud, if for no other reason, for fear of detection. The opportunity was not clear. But now upon some different point, he is tried. Whatever the form of temptation, then, it exists only when circumstances and inclination combine, and it will not assail the fortified but the weak point of your virtue. It will come where least expected, and your very lack of suspicion, your very self-confidence, may be its instrument. But wherever the evil wrestles with the good, be the strife ever so secret and personal, then you have need of the petition in the text.

I observe, in the next place, that every man has his peculiar temptation. One condition in life is really no more exposed than another. Yet, are we not apt to think otherwise? We may imagine that our condition is one of special trial, and that if we could only occupy our neighbor's sphere we should live better lives. This is all delusion. Our peculiar trials may not perplex the other, nor would his plague us; but, in his own situation each finds keen tests of virtue incident to that situation. The rich man has his temptations. Wrapped round with ease, and ministered to by obsequious circumstances, he is tempted to forget his dependence upon Divine help, to waste his life in splendid idleness, to weaken his soul with luxury and become confirmed in pride. He contemplates the robust health and diligent industry of the poor man, and, in a fit of sentimental regret, sighs for the safeguards of his condition. But were he actually to change places with the other and adopt his experience, he would learn that poverty has its temptations also. He would feel its fretful cares, its gloomy distrusts, its sense of weakness; and, too often, its social bitterness, its vulgar selfishness, and its coarse pleasures. Then he would understand how it was that the poor man used to look up to his estate, and sigh not merely for its material advantages, but for its freedom from evil suggestions. He would understand how it was that the poor man did not lay the blame of his sins where he should, upon *himself*, but upon his *circumstances*. So has the busy man of the world his peculiar temptations, his perplexing cares, his close, hot contacts with evil. So has the scholar his doubts and morbid suggestions. So has each man, I repeat, his own spiritual trials, so are all conditions pregnant with temptation, and if in either of these we fall the guilt is in ourselves; if in either of these we stand that victory is the noblest result we are permitted to achieve.

Once more; let us consider the instruction and the help which we derive from the fact that the personal history of Christ himself is, in respect to temptation, representative of our own. It is so, because, although he committed no sin, he was tempted *as we are*. But more than this—he was tempted *in all points* as we are. And we shall find, I think, that the three attempts upon his spiritual integrity, were in the three grades, or spheres, in which temptation assails us. Each temptation touched a different point in his condition; and, although the specific forms of our trial are innumerable, they may all be generalized in three great classes.

The first appeal of evil to the Savior, was a suggestion to *appetite.* Hungering as he was, it said to him —"*Command that these stones be made bread.*" "Exert your miraculous powers for the gratification of your bodily wants." My friends, although the personages are far different, and there are no supernatural powers appealed to, is not this the general character of the first great temptation that salutes us? It is the lowest in our spiritual discipline, yet it is, perhaps, the most common of all. Evil addresses us first in our *sensual* being. It urges us to live merely as sensual creatures, to debase our higher nature, to pervert our nobler powers, in the gratification of animal lusts. Is not this one great circle of evil, one radical principle, out of which spring innumerable sins? And is not this the life that multitudes are really living? Fools of passion, slaves of sense, discrowned heirs of immortality, casting themselves into the kennel and the mire! And is not this, as it were, a perversion of miraculous powers to mean uses? If we look with spiritual discernment upon the drunkard's bloated face, the libertine's jaded eye, the epicure's disease and agony, is it not the most melancholy thought of all, that a man, made to walk erect in the glory of his undying nature, should thus reel under the weight and decrepitude of vice—that he should thus seal up those springs of spiritual power, and waste that wealth of intellect, and paralyze that moral freedom—

that with the infinite heaven of light and love spread all around him, he should thus shut himself in to darkness and corruption? Is there not need for him, is there not often need for us, to say as the Master said—" Man shall not live by bread alone"—does not draw his whole life from sensual and outward things, possesses not merely a sensual and outward life—" Man shall not live by bread alone, but by every word that proceedeth out of the mouth of God."

Jesus was next tempted to cast himself from a pinnacle of the temple, relying upon his *personal consequence* for supernatural help. When we take away the accessories of this scene, it really resolves itself into an appeal to *selfishness.* The Tempter said, virtually,—" Do as you will, the whole universe is for *you,* and will serve *you.*" And is not the excitement of self-consequence the second order of temptation in our spiritual experience? We have risen then above the commission of gross vices because they injure ourselves; and this motive is the main-spring of all our negative virtue. We do this or that good act, because it benefits ourselves; and this motive will account for all our positive virtue. And so, in this spiritual sphere, our whole existence is the current of a selfish aim, and all our endeavor is for selfish ends. We live as though the powers of nature were ordained solely for ourselves; were merely to pamper and to serve us. We forget our relations to the rest —our stewardship as recipients of a common bounty—and so, if we are only happy and safe, we think not what our life is to others, we heed not their claims upon our sympathy and our service, we care for nothing but self. If we indulge in a luxury we think not that our present practice may induce moral death for our neighbor. What of him? If we are curtained about with comfort, we feel not that while we sleep he bleeds and perishes. What is that to us? Upon our pinnacle of self-will and vanity, we would, if we could, command the very laws of nature to bear us up, without regard to the general damage. Often, therefore, do we need to say to our hard and close-locked souls—"Thou shalt not tempt the Lord thy God."

The Tempter's last appeal was to *ambition*. "All the kingdoms of the earth will I give thee, if thou wilt fall down and worship me." And the highest grade of temptation in us, is connected with some earnest purpose, some intense, all-absorbing desire, to which we will sacrifice even the most sacred claims. This evil of ambition Milton has styled—

"The last infirmity of noble minds."

It is the source of those rarer and graver errors which appear in personal history. I say rarer, because they are generally exhibited by men of peculiar energy and peculiar worth. Such are far above the debasement of appetite, and although selfishness may mingle with their purpose, as it does with all wrong, that purpose is not inconsistent with many noble traits. But that purpose is also exclusive and uncompromising. It sets up its own object as the highest of all standards. It protrudes its own aim beyond all lawful limits. Hence men who would ordinarily spurn the wrong, when once the object of this intense desire glitters before them will thrust aside all sanctions, and serve even Satan to obtain it. Suppose, for instance, that a man sets his heart upon *wealth*. This is a lawful pursuit within due bounds, but he makes it the main end of life. Fond as he is of virtue in the ideal, nay practically honoring it in many points of his conduct, suppose that, to accomplish his purpose, one obstacle and only one stands in the way—but that involves truth, justice, virtue. Will not a conflict rise then in his soul? Will not temptation press him with a keen edge? Will he not labor to transform Satan into an angel of light that he may worship him?

If you would discover this kind of temptation operating in another form, you may behold a man of many rare qualities, become even a Napoleon in his single thirst for power. When the master desire is loose, what are burning cities, sacked dwellings, heaps of dead? Over all he looks straight to his object. He rides through the earth upon the pale horse of Death, its mane dripping blood. So, in a narrower scale, often, exists the same master passion. It burns in the bosoms of many who are neither vicious, nor merely selfish men. They thirst perhaps for the triumph of a sect, or a measure, or an opinion. Yes, this desire steals even into the calm atmosphere of the intellectual world. Even the so-called Truth-seeker, the professed disciple of "the first good and first fair," yields to its insinuations. How many inducements bribe him to shrink from the reality, to balk honest deductions, to forget his allegiance to the truth, to wrap himself in the mantle of pride, to swing into the dark gulf of skepticism! In clinging to his self-confident wisdom, may he not let go humility? In climbing the dizzy heights of knowledge, may he not reject the necessary help of faith?

But, whatever the shape of this temptation, it is the last and mightest, and therefore, to conquer it, we must take refuge in the last and mightiest power against all evil. We must "worship the Lord our God, and Him only must we serve."

These, then, are the radical spheres of temptation, out of which its ripe and multiform suggestions grow. And its force is victorious over us because we live only in ourselves and in immediate circumstances. We live impulsively, driven by appetite; we live subjectively, narrowing and drawing all things down to self; we live objectively, throwing away all things, even ourselves, to obtain, what is, after all, a secondary good. Let us, then, obey a higher law than lust. Let us look beyond ourselves. Let us bring the truth of God and of our own duty into relation with all we do. Let us rejoice, too, that we have not only the example of the Redeemer's struggles, but of his *victory*, and let us apply for his *spirit*. Let us implore the all-sufficient help of his Father and our Father—let us cry to Him in every time of moral need—"Lead us not into temptation!"

DISCOURSE VIII.

"But deliver us from evil."—Matthew vi: 13.

THIS is a spontaneous and universal petition. It is incident to every condition of hnman life. In one way or another it rises from every heart. Perhaps too it is the *earliest* of prayers. For, it may be questioned whether the desire for good is not first expressed by this deprecation of evil; whether man does not feel what he suffers before he knows what he wants; whether he does not struggle against the real before he perceives the ideal. Is not that sense of dependence, for instance, which induces all supplication, a sense of weakness? Is not the common cry—"Give us this day our daily bread," forced out by the pressure of necessity? Is not—"Forgive us our debts," the entreaty of a sharp remorse?

But, if not older, at least as old and as extensive as the desire for any good thing, is this prayer—"Deliver us from evil." It has been lifted up in all ages of the world, and wherever there is a consciousness of evil it rises against that evil. Against the earthquake and the tornado, against desolating flood and untimely frost, against conflagration and pestilence, against accident, disease, and death. The savage addresses it to his fetish, and the christian to his God. The devout man breathes it ere he goes among the unknown mischiefs and teeming possibilities of the day, or lies down to sleep with night and God around him. The sinner, in the shock of retribution deliriously shouts it to the Being whom he has so long forgotten. It is the child's prayer, who can picture the infinite Love only by images of parental affection, and who shrinks into that from a vague and chilling terror. It is the old man's petition who feels the props of life dropping away, and who fears lest second childhood should paralyze the faith of the first. It trembles upon the lips of youth just setting out to its venture. It yearns in the bosom of manhood, wrestling with difficulty and gathering its sheaves in the burden and heat of the day. Pitched in every key of distress, yet beating with one common undertone, from human hearts all round the earth, rises this great psalm of supplication.

I have separated the words of the text, then, from those which formed the subject of the last discourse, because, although they are closely connected, each is capable of a different signification from the other. The desire—"Lead us not into temptation," implies that the suppliant has some knowledge of himself and of moral relations; it indicates some depth of spiritual experience. The desire—"Deliver us from evil," as I have just said, is spontaneous. When we say—"Lead us not into temptation," we pray especially against ourselves, against the traitor within us. When we say—"Deliver us from evil," we pray against foreign ills also; against afflictions, against injuries that come without our own agency. Perhaps, we may say indeed, that one clause is the converse of the other. That one petition is *analytic*, and suggests the radical spring, the substantial reality of all evil; while the other is *synthetic*, and refers to evil in its various phases and modifications. "Lead us not into temptation," is a prayer breathed in the silence of introspection; "Deliver us from evil," is a prayer that breaks out in actual contact and suffering, in effort, and fear, and hope.

These are the reasons why I have set the text as a topic by itself. Let us now attend to some of the specific considerations which it suggests. Let us see what this prayer—"Deliver us from evil," implies; the state of mind and the conduct with which it is consistent.

I. It implies a recognition of the fact that what we usually term evil *is* evil. He who taught us to breathe this prayer did not inculcate *Stoicism*. His ideal of virtue was not a contemptuous endurance, too proud to stoop to calamity or to confess suffering. His religion does not seek to deaden our emotions, and to harden our fibres into rock. It acknowledges our humanity. It justifies our sensitiveness to pain and loss. Indeed, the *harshness* and *isolation* in the character of the Stoic, do not comport with the character of the Christian. The unflinching, impenetrable man is not lovely. Nor, on the other hand, can he love much. For, ere he could acquire this calm insensibility, he must curdle all the genial flow of his nature. He must break many affinities which connect him with his race. He must not only cauterize his own wounds, but destroy the very springs of sympathy. By killing the nerves of feeling, he not only suspends that mysterious ordinance by which our sharpest sufferings are involved with our richest enjoyments, but he cuts himself loose from the experiences of our humanity. He cannot respond to its emotions, nor understand its sentiments. He cannot mix with it in pity, and charity, and mutual help. The man of large love is always the man of deep sensibility. The man of broad and genial wisdom is a man controllable by human affections, and whose nature, at a thousand points, feels and shrinks from suffering. Nor is this sentiment inconsistent wiih the virtues of moral heroism and patience. Moral heroism is a different thing from philosophical contempt. It appears in resistance and in struggling, and while it is victorious over evil it denotes a keen appreciation of it. Patience is something more than physical endurance; it is spiritual resignation. It is not self-sufficiency, but filial reliance. It includes the feeling as well as the bearing of evil, and its essential excellence consists in this fact. While, beneath the light of God's countenance, its aspect is calm as the stilled waters of Galilee, its depths are yet tremulous with the agitation of the storm. I repeat, then, Christianity is not stoicism. But its rarest qualities, instead of indicating a stern insensibility to evil, grow out of a vivid realization of it.

I remark moreover that the system to which the sentiment of the text belongs, does not perplex our perception of evil. I mean by this, that Christianity gives us no hint that evil is only *apparent*—the reverse side of a fact the obverse of which is good—the unsubstantial shadow of a blessed purpose, hideous to our limited vision, but beautiful in the all-comprehending sight of God. This idea, therefore, at the strongest, is but a surmise, and, as I think, it is not a reasonable surmise. So far as circumstantial ills and bodily afflictions are concerned, such as poverty, disease, pain, death, I admit the blessed ends which they often serve. I would not deny the great fact that such evil is *disciplinary*—that good evolves from it. But, surely, the good *result* is not identical with the evil *agent*. Nor can I conceive that, from any point of view, the latter will be entitled to share the epithets of the former, or will change its apparent character. Rather may we believe that it accomplishes its disciplinary work, because it *is* essentially evil. Its intrinsic smart and sting constitute the very trial by which the human spirit is refined.

But, however we may regard these physical and earthly ills, much more objectionable is the notion I am now alluding to, in its application to *moral* evil—the notion that *sin* is one thing to man and another thing in the sight of God; that, as it revolves through the depths of our consciousness, it is *wrong*, but, as it turns in the light of his Omniscience, it is *right*. I cannot believe there is any such oblique puzzle in the universe; that there is any such ambiguity in the nature and the declarations of the Infinite One; but that moral evil *is* evil, above, and beneath, and to the core. If it is in any sense good, how could we pray to be delivered from it? It cannot be, then, that it is God's disguised servant. It is His open enemy. He does not work *with* it, but *against* it. He calls upon man to hate it, to resist it, to lift up his heart and voice against it—and He will be near to help.

The prayer of the text, then, implies the recognition of essential evil. Suffering by it as we do, it is right to pray that we may be delivered from it. It is right to pray that we may be delivered from *physical* and *earthly* woes. Such a prayer does not indicate ignorance of the good result which these evils serve. It is not a murmuring against the will of God. It is simply the shrinking of our human nature from actual suffering and injury—an earnest and filial desire, if it be God's pleasure, that these ills may be removed, or may not come. It is not for man to choose the path through which his Father shall lead him, but if, peradventure, that Father would ordain otherwise, he desires it may be so. At any rate, these woes oppress and hurt him, and he beats against them until he knows *what* the Supreme Will is. He does not recognize them as intrinsically otherwise than evil, and deems it not wrong to ask deliverance from them. Our common afflictions are treated as evils by the great Redeemer, and he pitied and removed them as such. His miracles were miracles of relief from earthly and bodily ills; they answered and thus sanctioned the prayers lifted against these ills. He mingled his sympathy with our human desires when he touched the blind eye, and the withered limb. He justified our prayers for rescue from sickness, when he laid his hand upon the fevered brow. He showed that it is not wrong to cry out against hunger, when he fed the five thousand. He made it proper for us to supplicate deliverance from the elements, when he stilled the wind and subdued the angry waters. And he consecrated our household affections that dread the death of the beloved; that will weep over their pale faces and bleed when we lay them away; he consecrated these feelings when he restored Jairus' daughter and the widow's son. More than all, we cannot forget that he himself wrestled in the gloom of the garden, and prayed that the cup might be taken from his lips. I repeat, then, it is right, in the loneliness of our closets and in the midst of the congregation, in the family circle, on the land and on the sea, to pray against these earthly ills—against poverty, disease, accident, and all that hurts us.

But let me say, that especially is this a prayer against *moral* evil. It is so in the connection in which it stands with the petition against temptation, and by the proper rendering of the text, which is—"Deliver us from the *evil one.*" "Deliver us from the principle of evil; from all sin and wrong, in whatever shape it comes." He who sincerely breathes this prayer, is penetrated by a profound conviction of the extent of vice, crime, falsehood, and all forms of iniquity. He sees this evil principle circulating through all the veins of the world—in institutions and governments, in customs and religions, in communities and individuals, and, especially, imbedded in his own heart, clinging to his own inner nature.

Thus beholding with a comprehensive and intense vision, he prays—"Deliver us from evil." No doubt this kind of evil eclipses all others, and it is this, therefore, that I shall generally refer to in the remainder of this discourse.

II. I proceed to remark that we do not practically apply this prayer by wholly *abstracting* ourselves from evil. There have been those in the world who have reasoned thus;—"Here," said they, "is the great fact of evil. It seems inherent in our mortal condition. It is inseparable from human nature and earthly circumstances. It encounters us wherever we go. It entangles us at every step. It meets us on the right hand and on the left. It stirs in the suggestions of appetite. It betrays us in our emotions. It is subtly involved with our affections. It taints and biasses our will. It bribes our reason. It is in the lust of the flesh, the pride of the eye, and the pride of life. How, then, shall we treat this fact? How shall we act concerning it?" Their answer has been;—"We must, as far as possible, close up all the avenues through which it suggests itself. We must retire from the outward world, shut ourselves in cloisters, mortify these fleshly powers, and, as far as possible, abandon the earth, rise above it by meditation and ecstasy." Such ideas as these have by no means been rare in the world. Those who have acted strictly upon them have been numerous and influential in the Christian Church. But I presume none who now hear me are likely to adopt these notions literally; and I would observe, therefore, that, in a modified form, they may be and are quite prevalent. At least two separate notions composing the main idea now alluded to are quite prevalent. The one, is that there is nothing but evil in our earthly circumstances; and the other, is the idea that it is of no use to contend with that evil. The name applied to this system in its combined and literal form is *Mysticism*, and adapting the same name to these separate phases, I observe that *mysticism* is no more sanctioned by christianity than stoicism. In the first place, it is not true that there is nothing but evil in the circumstances of the flesh and the world. I allude especially now to *moral* evil; for no man will deny the physical good involved in these. As to our sensual affections, then, I would say that they are to be kept in their proper sphere; they are to be resisted when they break beyond it; but no doubt they have a proper sphere. In that sphere, if they possess no character of moral goodness, they are not intrinsically evil. But we may give them an evil ascendency as much when we submit them to a minute scrutiny and vigilance, as when we serve them in blind indulgence. Nor let us, in any degree, cherish the Manichean heresy that the outward world, that matter, is intrinsically vile. In itself, it is God's creation—the theatre of His marvellous works, the temple of His all-pervading spirit. It bears the impress of His hand, it glows with divine beauty, it is the varied mold of His thought. What it becomes to us, depends upon what we are in ourselves. It may inflame our passions and deceive our judgment. It may be the arena of our lust and our hate. It may be the end of our desires. It may be the sarcophagus of our souls. But, to the good heart and the clear mind, it is a teacher of the most sacred wisdom, and an opportunity for the noblest labor. Such an one diligently pursuing the career of duty, finds glorious instruction upon its unrolled pages, and innumerable helpers in its various instruments.

In truth, moral evil is in the soul; in its attributes and affections; not in things without, not in the body or the world. If we shut up the portals of sense, we are still accessible to sin. If we build monastic walls as high as the firmament between ourselves and the outward world, still, the tempter and the snare are within us—in our thoughts, in our prayers, in our visions of heaven. No doubt, bad suggestions will come to us through the body. No doubt, sin lurks in the street and the field. But where will evil not intrude? Not in shrinking from it, but in contact with it, by God's help, we can best overcome it. Compelled to meet it everywhere, in that very encounter if we sincerely pray—"Deliver us from evil," there is an opportunity to weaken and to vanquish it. We subdue appetite not by seeking to eradicate it, but by exercising holy affections in spite of it. Not in shrinking from the world, but by doing our duty in it, do we blunt the edge of its temptations. Thus all things will help rather than hinder us, and we shall be made strong not weak, approved victors not timid deserters from the battle of life.

I have spoken of this error, because, I repeat, in one form or another I believe it is widely prevalent. Mingling with our religious feelings and theories, is the idea that the flesh and the world are utterly vile, that nature is half-infidel, that the common air has a taint, that social relations are allurements from holiness, that all earthly enjoyment is compromise with sin, and that religion, in fact, peculiarly consists in the renunciation of these and in retirement from them. That this is not a practical application of the prayer—"Deliver us from evil," I have yet farther to show in the sequel of this discourse.

Upon the other branch of Mysticism, I shall speak but briefly; the idea that it is of no avail to contend with evil. We may detect its legitimate conclusions in that skepticism which affirms the total depravity and helplessness of the race, which denies all progress, and, in fact, not only deprecates moral action, but strikes at the root of morality itself. We may detect it also in that selfish conservatism which pleads against any attempt at reform, and makes a profitable use of its philosophy. In neither of these is the doctrine or hope of the petition contained in the text. He who prays—"Deliver us from evil," strives against it, and believes in the possibility of its removal.

III. I observe, again, that we do not make a practical application of this prayer when we live in moral *indifference*, when we make no resistance to evil, but habitually indulge it. In other words, if the Christian idea is not expressed in Stoicism, nor Mysticism, it certainly is not consistent with *Epicureanism.* And in this form more than any other, the petition is virtually disregarded. Many men—are we not compelled to say *most?*—while they shrink from physical ill, so far from avoiding the contact of moral evil, live heedlessly with it and in it. A great portion of them are not violent sinners. They are not criminal, nor grossly vicious. But they are morally insensible. They have no inward perception, no spiritual ideal of life. They do not realize the claims of duty, the great end of being, and their immortal relations. The charmed circle of the world hems them around, and their souls are entangled and absorbed in its realities. Or if, for a moment, the veil of sense breaks away, and they catch glimpses of the starry infinitude about them, it soon closes again, and their thoughts, affections, hopes, are all as secular as ever. Now this insensibility to spiritual good, and, therefore, to spiritual evil, I call Epicureanism. True, it has various aspects. It appears in the atheistic scoffer and the shrewd man of the world; in the voluptuary and the utilitarian.

You might behold it in one form, should you pass to-night through the streets of this great city, and enter its haunts of debauchery, its dens of shame. No doubt, you would find there some one to whom this world is but a theatre of sensual indulgence; whose only ideal of good is pleasure, and that pleasure the evanescent thrill of animal enjoyment. To whom this Sabbath has brought no holy associations, no spiritual opportunities, no auroral light of immortality; but who has used it as a season of vicious indulgence, or a carnival of revelry and lust. And this phase of Epicureanism you may discover thickly around you, in degrees more or less refined. Under the form of swinish excess, or the mask of a polished libertinism, you may see men who live "as the brutes that perish;" whose golden sands of life are running away in base and frivolous uses; who hasten to quench the suggestions of appetite in sottish inebriety, or artfully prolong them that they may tease satiety into zest; to whom the present is a game of chance and the future a blank, the Bible a fable, and the universe godless; to whom, perhaps, even now, life's feast seems about to close; who find the lights going out and themselves trembling with decay, yet who strain the lees of the tasteless wine, and crown themselves with the withered garlands, and say with a glee unnatural as laughter among the tombs—"Let us eat and drink, for to-morrow we die!"

But, my friends, there are other forms of Epicureanism, and while we shrink from it in this phase, are we sure that we ourselves do not exhibit it in some other? Not merely the gross sensualist or the skeptical philosopher, but, I repeat, the man whose whole soul is bound up in earthly interests; who under many respectable moralities, and professions of religion even, seeks only a sensual and selfish end; who has no communion with God and his own soul, or into whose most sacred hours intrudes the jar and hum of the world; who has no vigilant conscience, no clear moral sense, no infinite aspirations; this man, also, is an Epicurean. As his conception of life does not include the highest good, he is not conscious of the profoundest evil. He may have employed the prayer of the text in a crisis of bodily suffering, a dread of some physical calamity, or with a vague religious emotion. But it has never sprung from depths of spiritual earnestness and agony. He has never detected the clinging subtlety of sin, he has never felt the burden of guilt, he has never experienced the fiercest edge of temptation, or wrestled with it in the solitude of his own soul; and, therefore, the cry—"Deliver us from evil," is not expressed by him in its profoundest sense. Neither in this, nor in any other degree of Epicureanism, of mere sensual life, of moral unconsciousness, can this prayer be consistently uttered.

Yet, is it not strange that men should live so? That so little consideration should be given to our inward being, and the real end of existence? If the universe in which we are placed, if our own natures, have any high and holy meaning; if the suggestions of truth, and beauty, and goodness that visit us in our rarest moments are not as delusive as the phantasms that haunt a sick man's dream; if we are not mere floats upon a dead sea, but voyagers upon an ever-flowing river; if we are embosomed in any wonder; if the discipline of earth has any consistent purpose; if the pulses of another life throb mysteriously with this; if we are heirs of immortality, and not mere denizens of the market and the charnel-house; if the Bible fits any mood of our joy or sorrow; if the advent and the sufferings of Jesus make any appeal to us; then let us throw off this fettering and torpid worldliness; let us perceive that "spiritual interests are real and supreme;" let us pray to be delivered from this evil of practical unbelief, and then we shall be aware of, we shall strive against and overcome all other forms of evil.

IV. If the prayer of the text is not consistent with a stoical contempt for evil, a mystical abstraction from it, or an epicurean indulgence in it, then it comports with a distinct *recognition* of it, a courageous *contact* with it, and a devout *struggle* against it; and these elements consist with the Christian idea of evil. He who fully expresses the significance of this petition, prays against something which he *feels* and *acknowledges*. He is not wrapped about with any impenetrable robe of philosophy; he has not drugged his humanity. He confesses its liabilities and its wants. His flesh quivers with pain. He shrinks from the piercing wind and the heat. He deprecates sickness and loss, and "the stings and arrows of outrageous fortune." He does not presumptuously confront death. He perceives the chastening ministry of these ills, and when they fall upon him seeks to improve the discipline; but he does not deny their essential evil. While his petition consists with a clear recognition of his responsibility, of the work he must do in his own behalf, it is mingled with faith in an instant and universal Providence. While this recoil from adversity is not the expression of cowardice, or hypocondria, it quickens in his heart a large sympathy for all other men, for they are, like himself, weak, exposed, suffering. But chiefly does he pray against moral evil, keenly realizing its influence in his own soul, and its power throughout the world. Moreover, while he is aware that this most dreadful wo of all meets him in every part of the world, springs a snare upon him in every opportunity, and steals inio his nature through countless avenues of temptation, he does not seek to extirpate that nature or to fence himself in from that world. But, rather, in the fields of ordinary life, in the ever-widening circle of daily duties, he detects the agents of his moral help, and he prays for holy affections and firm faith, that, wherever he encounters this manifold evil, he may disarm it, and drive it away, and fill its place with blessings. He does not deny the good there is in our human lot, and the share we may lawfully have in the amenities of our lower estate; but he leaps from the laxity of self-indulgence, he shrinks from drowsy contact with sin, he beats and strives against it with the energy of an awakened conscience and the enthusiasm of a spirtual aim.

This, then, is the idea of evil which blends with the Christian's prayer—this is a general definition of his views and his conduct. But, as I close, let me add to this description some specific suggestions which we must heed if we would consistently utter this petition. First then, let me distinctly re-iterate the fact that, if we would truly breathe this prayer, we must realize that there is a far deeper than any earthly evil. Let us not fix our ideal of happiness in the gratification of the senses, in deliverance from temporal ill. Let us remember that keener than poverty is barreness of soul, that richer than houses and lands is a spirit fortified against sin. That no disappointment, loss, hunger, is like a guilty conscience and an alienated heart.

Again; let not the words before us be the *only* prayer we use. I mean by this, let us not apply to God merely in our adversity and our danger. How many there are who do this, whose whole conception of Religion is that of a charm or rescue, and is associated only with the darker phases of human life! This prayer can consistently rise, not from a frightened, but from an habitually devout spirit, from one who utters and understands all the sentiments of the Lord's Prayer.

Nor, let this prayer be with us the language of a peevish discontent, or an indolent restlessness. Let us not be too ready to say—"Deliver us from evil," as the expression of our desire to escape from the condition in which we are placed. Let us consider how much of that evil depends upon our own agency, and that we shall be delivered from it no where without our own effort. That the ruggedness of our lot, is the noblest opportunity for our endeavor, and that the nature of any circumstances depends much upon the spirit with which we live among them.

Remember, again, that this is a *hopeful* petition. This cry "Deliver us from evil," bursting from the sincere heart of humanity is a call that God hears and has heard for six-thousand years. It has come from saintly souls, from true martyrs and reformers—and he has heard it. It is breathed in all the efforts for human progress, and he hears it. It is a cry with which the whole creation groaneth and travaileth, and he hears it. However independent our agency may be, let us not forget his nature and the promise of his help.

And, once more, let us consider the *fraternal* character of this petition. It does not say—"Deliver *me*," but "Deliver *us*." Wherever we breathe it, then, whatever our individual wants, it comprehends with these the needs and the woes of humanity. Religion always lifts us up from a narrow selfishness and carries us out into the universal. Would it not, I ask you, enlarge our thoughts—would it not take us abroad from our own joys and sorrows, would it not quicken our sense of the brotherhood of the race,—to reflect from how many postures of humanity the cry—"Deliver us from evil," is this moment rising? Consider that, even as I speak, it circles the round earth and peals up to heaven from churches and cathedrals, from sainted closets and family altars, from the philanthropist over his schemes, from the bosom of the tempted, from the penitent gush of confession, from the sick man scared by incongruous dreams and waking to the reality of pain, from homes whence even the Sabbath's peace cannot exorcise the gaunt face of poverty, from the muffled arteries of cities jarring with guilt and wo, from the bleak wilderness where the traveller sinks worn out and lost, from the ship where the gale is straining the naked masts and the white waves dash to the shivering stars. I ask would it not lessen our own sorrows, would it not quicken our sympathy and our diligence, if we should breathe this prayer remembering the broad field and the multiform evil about us, and considering how many with us are lifting the same cry to heaven?

But on the other hand, let not any expanded hopes or fraternal sympathies, let not any general application of this petition, draw us away from its individual purpose. If we pray against evil in the world at large, let us not fail to seek its removal from our own souls. If we labor to drive it from community, let us strive to exorcise it from our own hearts. For only out of this inward, personal salvation, can the wide circle of human regeneration flow. And both by supplication and labor let us exhibit the true ideal of all prayer. By action and by entreaty let us continually say—"Deliver us from evil."

DISCOURSE IX.

"For thine is the kingdom, the power, and the glory, forever. Amen." —Matthew vi : 13.

The authenticity of this Doxology is denied by the best critics, and it is not subjoined to the Lord's Prayer as found in the Gospel of Luke. It is consecrated, however, by the most ancient usage, and has become so incorporated with the original formula as to share in all its sacred associations. But, besides this, there is an intrinsic harmony between the ascriptions of the text and the preceding sentences. They fitly close the prayer, so that it ends as it begins—with God. They declare the grounds of our supplication, and of our worship. And although they may express only what has before been implied, yet our faith is strengthened and our devotion made more intense by this concentration of our feelings and this re-collection of our thoughts. In accordance with these suggestions, I propose to occupy a portion of this discourse with a consideration of the words now before us, and to devote the remainder to some concluding remarks upon the whole prayer.

"For thine is the *Kingdom.*" This is the first ascription. And it *must* be the first, not only here but in all circumstances. It proclaims the great truth that there is in the universe a perpetual AUTHORITY and an all-pervading CONTROL; that in the material and the spiritual worlds nothing is at loose ends; but everywhere there is a sacred order, an intelligible tendency, and a fixed result. And this is the dominion of the Infinite Creator, Benefactor, and Father.

His is the Kingdom of *Nature.* In Him is the centre of all its affinities and the secret of its involutions. Upon Him depend all its orders of being. He touches its springs. From His hidden depths flows out its universal life. And after all the uses to which man can compel it, after all the knowledge he can obtain and all the definitions he can construct, are we not obliged to say that God's *sovereignty* is the final interpretation of nature, and that its profoundest manifestations are the express witnesses of this? What better can we say than that "heaven is His throne, and earth His footstool?" that the laws of matter are the stereotyped publications of His will. That the pomp of the seasons, the out-goings of the morning and the evening, the universal flush of beauty, are the indefinable expressions of His joy? In the catacombs of buried epochs, in hieroglyphics of rock, we read the archives of his solitary doings when no man was upon the earth. And as we explore the starry infinitudes around us, as we go forth among worlds swarming thicker than summer leaves, and ask—"Why this illimitable splendor, this profusion of being?" what answer can we obtain except—"Such is God's will and way?" These are the shining vassals of his purpose, the burning wheels of His continuous plan—for His is the Kingdom.

His, too, is the Kingdom of the *spiritual* world, the world of moral action, of the individual soul, of all intelligent beings from the angels who cast their crowns at His feet to the child who springs into life and wonder. Although man hangs upon the poise of his own moral nature, and acts in the orbit of his own free-will, the sphere of his agency is not isolated from God. The infinite Spirit that induces the motion and quickens the pulses of blind matter, is surely in communion with its own image and essence. In some way—we cannot pretend to know how—He harmonizes our freedom with His control. He reigns in the individual soul also, by the power of motives and the pressure of authority; those motives being the attractions of absolute *Goodness*, and that authority the sovereignty of absolute *Right*. And that which is manifest in the individual, is manifest in the race, in its phases, and in its whole career. In the sanctions of law and government, by which "Kings reign and princes decree justice;" in the exhibition of a central stability apparent amid all changes; in the vindication of eternal principles, in the great fact of human progress; in the silent and unconscious order into which even the most promiscuous events fall; we detect the gulf-stream of His Providence, and discover that God reigns in history.

His Kingdom is in the physical and the spiritual worlds then. In our grandest sweeps of vision we see each of these facts, and comprehend the essential unity of the two. In the calm planet and the falling sparrow, in the moral awards and unfolding mysteries of human life, in the breaking waves of ages and the crumbling of earthly thrones, we realize that there is a universal and eternal dominion, and only one. It is His to whom we say—"Thine is the Kingdom;" deriving from that truth both confidence to pray, and reasons to adore.

And His, also, is the *Power*. Possessing the dominion, He is able to maintain it. It is His creation; and He who constructed the universe can control its grandest movements and its minutest parts. As there is no contingency beyond His forethought, so there is no want beyond His resources. Through all the channels of this great whole He pours continual sustenance. The phenomenon of material Force itself, in the last analysis, can only be defined as the immediate effect of His contact, the uncoiling energy of His will. And as, apart from His action, therefore, we cannot form any conception of the essential character of power and motion, we recognize the sublime truth of the Hebrew axiom, that 'Force is God." The feeling of dependence in the soul of every man is a witness to the same truth. Not only does He minister to all inferior things, but He refreshes the springs of our human agency. He gives us our daily bread by giving us the faculties to obtain it. He is the Life of all intellect, the Source of all knowledge. And how often would the soul perish in its moral necessities without His succor and His mercy! And while this truth should prevent forgetfulness, and keep us humble, it should also sōothe and encourage us. Does it not excite our devotion and strengthen our filial trust, to look beyond all these circling forms of being to the Almighty deep in which we are embosomed, to the calm Omnipotence that hems us in, to that spring of original energy which gushes in the heart of all things, and thus, at the close of a prayer in which so many wants have been expressed, to feel and say—"Oh God! thine is the *Power*."

His is the *Glory*. He who has the Kingdom and the Power, exercises them for the best ends. All that is needed, all that is good, is His gift. Therefore, let Him have the praise. Let thanksgiving crown our supplication. Let us continually acknowledge the benefits He confers. His is the glory, of *the works* He performs. When, of old, Moses asked to see that glory, He said—"I will make all my *Goodness* pass before thee." And that exhibition of His glory is always unfolding to us. His, too, is the glory of His *own intrinsic Excellence*, so that they who see Him the clearest glorify Him most. The Uncreated is illustrated in all His creation. That which makes the perpetual noon of heaven, shines in every ray of earth. That which belongs to the Infinite Spirit is reflected in the soul of man. His is the glory, inherent, original, and alone. Let us by the fact that this glory is manifested in works of mercy, be encouraged to ask what we need. Let us rejoice that we can become conscious of our own spiritual nature in our adoration of spiritual Excellence, in our privilege of mingling our worship with the sea of bliss and harmony that rolls before His throne, and that, at the close of our feeble, earthly prayer, we may reiterate the strain which sweeps downward from heaven and fills the universe. For we too can say—"Thine is the Glory."

And, having thus uttered these ascriptions, we remember that He to whom we render them, possesses these attributes *eternally*. He is the unchangeable God.

His Kingdom is a never-ending Kingdom. His Power is exhaustless. His Glory is infinite. In order that there may be any consistent thought and action, it is necessary that we should have a conviction of something *permanent* in the universe; of everlasting *being* subsisting as the *basis* of all these flying phenomena. In a time like the present especially, when all theories are set adrift and all questions agitated, how necessary is it that we should be convinced that there is *everlasting* Truth. When sceptred authority is broken and the stability of all government is shaken by the eager rush of revolution, how much do we need to believe in an *immutable* moral control. And while science draws the veil from the primeval earth, and shows us the wrecks of successive epochs, and prophecies the funeral-pyre of suns and systems, how sublime is it to feel the beating pulses of illimitable Love, to confide in Him to whose spirit we are allied, and who will maintain us in being through all material changes. And is it not the bliss and the miracle of prayer, that it lifts us away from our sins, our little cares, our teasing wants, and all the mutations of earth, and embosoms us in the communion of the Eternal. Does it not give strength, and meaning, and blessedness to our devotions, then, when we say—"For thine is the kingdom, the power, and the glory, *forever.*"

And thus employing these ascriptions as reasons for our devotion, and reflecting their light back upon the whole Prayer which we have been considering; seeing what we have asked, what we have offered, and to Whom our devotion has been addressed; let it have the confirmation of our whole soul—let us seal it with our solemn *"Amen!"*

And that the conviction thus expressed may be still more clearly confirmed, I pass to the second division of my discourse, for the purpose of offering some general remarks upon the whole Prayer. I have time, however, for but two or three specifications, but I earnestly commend this Formula to your own study, that by familiarity with it you may be able to discern characteristics which I can but imperfectly suggest, or must leave untouched.

I. I would direct your attention to the consistency of this prayer, to the natural evolution of its sentences. It is not a promiscuous collection of petitions and ascriptions, but it is an organic whole. One clause follows the other in a necessary order. This I have shown, from time to time during the series. But it is a fact sufficiently important to urge upon your attention again, and it is more intelligible when the whole Prayer lies before us. I repeat, then, the succession of topics in this prayer is a natural one. It accords with our spiritual experience. Of course I do not maintain that we can never pray in any other order; for we may at times take one point in this prayer and dwell almost exclusively upon it. For a season its sentiment may be so prominent in our souls, that it *will* come first. But I am speaking now of this as a model of devotion, and I say that, as such, it expresses the way in which our devout thoughts and feelings are naturally unfolded.

First of all, we say, "*Our Father* which *art in heaven.*" And, surely, belief in God must stand before every other sentiment. God must be the Being whom we address. Were there no Deity the idea of prayer would not exist. But we must have right conceptions of God; and ere we can say, "*Hallowed be thy name,*" we must know *what* that name is. And having attained the conception of the Father, this sentiment breaks spontaneously from our hearts, as the expression of reverent and filial homage. We heartily desire clearer manifestations of Him, and that we may more consistently honor Him. But God's name will not be universally hallowed, until His dominion is universally felt and acknowledged. In order, then, that He may be known as the Father and adored as the God of all,—in order that the blessedness of His rule may extend through all hearts, we pray: "*thy kingdom* come!" But all devout knowledge and worship of God, involves a desire that He may reign not only as He actually does reign, in the power of His universal control, but also in the voluntary obedience of His moral offspring. And, moreover, all such worship and knowledge must consist with effort on our part to advance that reign. In close connection, then, with our desire for the coming of God's Kingdom, we pray, "*thy will be done on earth as it is in heaven;*" for thus we express our conception of the real method through which His Kingdom must come. This petition throws us upon our personal responsibility; but while we know how much we resist the divine will, and therefore how much we ought to *do*, we perceive in how many ways that will works irresistibly, and, therefore, how much we must *endure;* and we learn that by resignation, as well as by action, may His Kingdom be advanced in our own souls and in the souls of all men. These great moral desires will rise first in a devout mind; and those which are more general, springing up in the contemplation of God's Excellence, will be uttered before those which are more private and particular. But the consideration of God's Will, leads us to remember His power: the consciousness of our freedom suggests our limitation, and the necessities with which we struggle; and so we lift one petition for temporal good, and cry, "*Give us this day our daily bread.*" But quickly do our material wants suggest our spiritual necessities; quickly do mercies received remind us of mercies neglected, of our ingratitude and our guilt: quickly does the hunger of the body illustrate the hunger of the soul, and to our great Benefactor, whom we have forgotten and disobeyed, we exclaim, "*Forgive us our debts,*" and learn how essential to the spirit and purpose of this prayer it is that we should "*forgive our debtors.*" And who that has ever sincerely uttered this petition for pardon, has not shrunk with fear and shame from the exposures of the world without and from his own weakness within, and cried, "*Lead us not into*—abandon us not to—*temptation?*" and with a sense of all his dangers, but especially of the peril in his own heart, added—"*Deliver us from evil?*" Thus having breathed the sentiments of the soul in a natural order, we confirm all these utterances by the Doxology. "Accept this homage," we say, "grant these requests," "*For thine is the Kingdom, the Power, and the Glory, forever, Amen.*"

I do not present this as a complete analysis of these sentences, or as exhibiting every point suggested. I am aware too that in the diversities of individual feeling and circumstance, they may have a varied application, but I make this recapitulation to illustrate the consistency and mutual relation of the topics in the Prayer; and I believe that he who breathes it in its essential significance, will generally find that it corresponds to the unfolding of his spiritual experience, to the order in which devout desires and feelings rise in his soul.

II. Consider the *comprehensiveness* of this Prayer. If it corresponds to the order of our spiritual experience, then, of course, it must contain all the great requisites of devotion. And, upon examination, we see that it does. We might infer this, indeed, from the circumstances under which it was first uttered. It was given as a model of Prayer. We are told in Luke, that Christ taught it in compliance with the request of his disciples —" Lord, teach us how to pray." And in Matthew, he says " *When* ye pray, say, our Father." As a model, then, we might expect to find in it all the elements of devotion. We should not expect to find in it all the multiform combinations of these elements, or a dilated expression of them, such as we may need in the experiences of every-day life. Nor are we confined to the precise words before us. There may be times when we shall be able to say nothing else. There may be times, too, when our thoughts are so clear and our desires so compact, that we find the best vehicle for our devotion in this literal expression. But they understand but little of the human spirit in its devout experiences who would limit it to just these sentences. Certainly, the example of Christ does not teach this. He prayed as circumstances suggested, or his spirit moved. So is it with us. There are times when no form will suffice; when it would restrain and break our devotion; when it would not give us the relief we need, nor express the burden of our souls. There are occasions when no litany, however comprehensive in its elements or varied in its applications, can do this, and not even the mere language in the Lord's Prayer; but the devout sentiment bursting from the heart, must come fittest to the circumstance, spontaneously, gushing in a full and unrestricted tide. The mother by the sick-bed of her child cannot command her feelings, so as merely to say—"Deliver us from evil." The famishing man cannot stop short with—"Give us this day our daily bread." The returning sinner must pour out his penitence in more words than "Forgive us our debts." There may be, there will be, circumstances in private and public devotion, when some particular sentiment in this Prayer will be longer dwelt upon and more pressingly urged. I am not advocating prolixity in devotion. I know what Christ says of "much speaking," and of "vain repetitions;" though here evidently he condemns *mere* words, *vain* repetitions; but no where does he limit the flow of the earnest spirit to one mold of expression.

But while the precise language of this prayer is not to be considered as the sole expression of devotion, yet,

I repeat, as a model, it contains the essence of all sincere homage and supplication. There is nothing we *do* say that is not really implied here. The germs of every devout thought and desire are in these simple words. What more can you say of God than to style Him "Father?" How much better can you express worship than to say—"Hallowed be thy name?" In what way would you solicit His protection, that would imply more than—"Deliver us from evil?" How can you ask a higher good for your soul than by saying "Thy Will be done?" Is not the need for earthly good, expressed in the desire for "daily bread?" Is not the heaviest burden we bear relieved, when we sincerely cry—"Forgive us our debts?"

As a model of devotion, then, it is wonderful how this Prayer is adjusted to our spiritual experiences, and expresses all our sentiments and desires. Surely, it could have come only from one "Who knew what was in man." And even though fragments of it may be found in the Jewish liturgies, in its present construction it is original, and, as such, in its comprehensiveness and adaptation, it is an illustration and an evidence of Christianity.

But I would have you notice farther, as an instance of the comprehensiveness of this Formula, that *it really suggests all the great truths of Religion.* Implying the divine mission of Jesus, it proclaims the Existence, Paternity, and Providence of God, the spiritual nature of man, his sinfulness and dependence, the doctrines of repentance and forgiveness, and the brotherhood of the human race. Of course, we find these and other truths more distinctly and elaborately stated in other portions of the Gospel, but are they not essentially contained here? Heartily believing all that the Lord's Prayer implies, do we not possess the marrow of Christian doctrine? If this be so, we might better test the orthodoxy of men by the sincerity with which they utter this prayer, than by the logical definitions of a creed? For, language may misrepresent a man's meaning, his reasoning may be confused, but the sentiments he breathes in true devotion always express his deepest convictions, and reveal what he is really trying to say by his formulas and symbols. But if we think that the broad diversities of opinion which exist among the professed disciples of Jesus, cannot thus be reconciled, we must at least admit, that the universal usage of this prayer indicates an essential unity that is more vital than their antagonism. Whatever their variations of doctrine, it is certain that this manual is comprehensive enough to consist with them all, and in it all their differences melt into a common expression. Through every age of the church amid the uproar of sects, and the din of controversy, this prayer has gone up as the utterance of one undivided heart; and, when they will hear the beating of this sweet accordance, all Christians may recognize how identical are the Sources of their belief, and the Objects of their love. Even now, I repeat, it shows how closely related at the altar, are men widely separated by the dogma and the creed.

I will just allude to one more illustration of the comprehensiveness of this Prayer, and pass on to another topic. I mean its *adaptation to different periods and conditions of human existence.* I have said that it unfolds in the order of man's spiritual experience, but we must remember that this is an experience of diverse tone and intensity. While those great conceptions of God and His government, of need and weakness, of sinfulness and duty, will always animate a sincere utterance of this Prayer, those conceptions may rise in different elevations of the human soul, and indicate a greater or less compass of thought. This is a prayer for all ranks and conditions. For the multitude on the mountain and the Rabbi in the synagogue; for the penitent prodigal and the advanced saint; and it meets and conveys the experiences of each. The peasant finds in its simple sentences a vehicle for his homage and his wants, while the devout philosopher knows no form of utterance so pregnant. It is the first prayer the mother teaches, the first prayer that falters on the lips of the child; and it is so easy and so adaptive that he carries it through all the rough contacts of the world, along with the best memories of home. And nothing so fit as this can the man breathe from his lips, to purify his heart, to strengthen his good resolutions, and to confirm his hope, as he walks through the lengthening shadows and among the withered leaves, in the autumn of life.

III. Finally; let me urge the argument which this Prayer presents for *devotion* and a *devout life.* By constructing the *model,* Christ enjoined the *habit* of prayer, as he has done elsewhere both by precept and example. Yet this is not an arbitrary injunction. The form was made in answer to an earnest desire. But in thus appointing an expression for supplication and homage, Jesus did not merely meet the wants of his immediate disciples, but he has exposed a class of emotions, which, consciously or vaguely, stir in every human spirit. Prayer is natural. Every man has in him the elements of religion; folded up it may be in secularity and sin, unheeded and forgotten; yet, at times—in some hour of silent thought, or some shock of Providence—responding like a great deep to the highest realities of being; to the mysteries of God and immortality, of life and death. Oh! there is not one so hard, so reckless, drifted away so utterly from the current of humanity, as never to experience blessed desires, and more than earthly inflnences. There is not one who has not, at some period, felt the impulse and the necessity of prayer, and lifted up his cry to God as his helper. But the wonder is that these seasons are not more common, more habitual; that, living as we do in contact with the infinite God, wrapped around by his almighty Spirit, we should not feel it more. That, considering the magnificence of the universe about us—the varying loveliness of the day, the rolling splendors of the night, we should not gladly seize our privilege to pass within the veil and commune face to face with the Being who made it all. That, throbbing with the consciousness of filial dependence, we should not lean upon the arm of our everlasting Father. That, knowing our exposures, our follies, and our faults, we do not seek the succors of His Spirit, and the shield of His protection. That, with no intervening meditation, no sense of the invisible God, we should sink to the embrace of slumber and leap into the morning light; making our homes but inns of bodily refreshment, and all outside a mart of worldly care; as though life, embosomed as it is in wonder, breathing as it does with unseen influences, were but a flow of sensual interests, and "rounded with a sleep."

And yet it is so. Notwithstanding this religious consciousness in men, notwithstanding their spiritual necessities which they sometimes feel, there is a common neglect of devotion and a strange reluctance to engage in it. It would occupy more time than it is necessary to use, to exhibit all the reasons for this disinclination. No excuse which may be offered for it, will stand an honest examination for a moment; nay, the very excuse, it is likely, will only the more demonstrate the necessity for prayer. Do we plead unworthiness? is not, then, that petition—"Forgive us our debts," the very thing we need to utter? Do we fear that our prayers and our conduct would be inconsistent? will not habitual and sincere prayer make our best aspirations and our daily actions more at one? Or are we disposed to associate the practice of devotion with weakness and ridicule? Let only one clear thought of the realities involved in and implied by that practice, break upon us, and it will solemnize all our future life, and lift it above a trivial worldliness, and a practical atheism. Never is human nature so strong as when it leans upon God, never is its dignity so manifest as when man "bursts into the infinite and kneels."

Or, it may be said—"It is not *true* prayer that we neglect or dislike; but it is formality, it is superstitious observance, it is Phariseeism and cant." Of a deadening formality it is well for us to beware. We cannot too constantly remember that prayer is a *spirit* not a *form.* It is not essentially a motion of the lips but of the soul. It does not consist in articulate words but in earnest desires. And thus, no doubt, every heartfelt sentiment, expressed or unexpressed, may be a prayer. No doubt every diligent endeavor is one; and, in this sense, the husbandman prays when he turns up the furrows to the spring rains; in this sense the philosopher prays when he seeks after some great truth. But this is not the whole idea of prayer. For *that* is the conscious communion of our spirits with God's. It is the concentration of our souls in a special act. Not confined to words but often expressed in words; not limited to times and places, but assisted by these, and without some attention to these not likely to be exercised at all. Let us beware of all cant, too. Let us have no forced looks, no unreasonable constraints. Let us cherish the loftiest spiritual moods we may, and feel that everywhere and at all seasons, and in the most silent breathings of the soul, we can pray; but surely we must see that set times and vocal utterances are very efficient in producing such spiritual and habitual devotion; and therefore we have such a manual as the Lord's Prayer.

But there is a skeptical objection to prayer which it will be well to notice here, especially as it may help explain that reluctance to which I am now alluding. It is sometimes said—"What is the *use* of Prayer? Does it change God? Does it alter the laws of nature?" Now there are several answers to this interrogatory objection. In the first place, as I have shown, prayer is really a necessity of our nature, an instinctive impulse of the human soul towards God. This alone is an evidence that it has a use. It has been employed in all ages and in all lands, and nothing so instinctive and universal exists without a meaning and an end. Again, Prayer has a beneficial operation upon ourselves. Surely, I need not dwell upon illustrations of this—upon the benefit of communion with the best Being in the universe, upon the strength imparted by the exercise of faith which prayer implies, upon the practical blessedness of that spirit of forgiveness and penitence which we breathe. However much we may sink or go astray, prayer always lifts us to a higher mood, and sets our feet in the right path. If we habitually and sincerely utter it, it will transform and sanctify our lives.

But I deny the force of the argument suggested in the proposition that prayer cannot change God, nor alter the laws of nature. I do not say that prayer *can* effect either of these results. But I *do* say that a direct answer to prayer from God does not imply any change in Him, nor in His ordinances; but simply that in prayer a certain instrumentality is used upon the exercise of which certain results will follow, which would not ensue without the use of this instrumentality. If a man should pray that a harvest may spring up without any seed, he would utter a prayer to which he could not expect an answer. But who shall say that his prayer is not directly answered when he asks for *ability* to sow the seed? Who can determine the mysterious methods by which strength is imparted? Now it is an ordinance of God that the harvest shall depend upon the sowing of seed. If that instrumentality is not employed no result follows. But, still, the *possibilities* all exist whether the means are used or not. And should it have so happened that man had sowed the seed but once, contrary to all human experience, past and future, a harvest would have sprung up. But would this unusual fact have violated any law of nature? Certainly not. The strange result would have indicated simply a compliance with established terms, which compliance had not been previously rendered. So is it, as I conceive, with prayer. It is a spiritual instrumentality upon the employment of which certain results are contingent. And that God should grant peculiar and direct blessings upon the touching of that one spring, which He will give in no other way, is no more miraculous than that He should give the harvest when the seed is sown. To say that He grants answers to prayer as well as to labor, is only saying that man works with God and God with man in more ways than one. *How* He answers prayer is a mystery, but it is no more a mystery than the process which converts the kernel into the full corn in the ear—than the connection between thought and action—than the existence of God and the methods of His communication with the human soul.

But, after all, those who really cherish the spirit of devotion, find the best answer to all these cavils. Their immortal desires, their ever-recurring wants, their conscious weakness, is a sufficient argument for Prayer. Let us look into our own souls and we shall find it so. Let us consider all our condition, and heed the great suggestion to devotion which Christ has given us!

But I said not only that this prayer affords an argument for devotion, but for a *devout life*. This is no more than a reiteration of what I have frequently said in the delivery of these discourses; no more than a repetition of the truth that true prayer consists in action as well as aspiration. If the sincere utterance of these devout sentiments is necessary to all good conduct, neither can we consistently utter it without endeavoring to conform our conduct to its sentiments.

And consider, I beseech you, what must be the effect if we carry out the spirit of this prayer. If we should live in and from that spirit, how would life, and duty, and our fellow-men, and our souls, and God appear to us? If this Prayer expresses the true order of al. spiritual experience; if it comprehends all the great truths of Religion; then does it contain all the elements of a good life. And as I now draw these discourses to a close which for so many Sabbath evenings have required my labor and your attention, I know not that I could make a more fitting appeal than to urge you so to study this prayer as to understand it, so to understand it as to heartily and daily breathe its sentiments, so to breathe its sentiments as to make them living springs of action in your souls, as to re-present them in all youı lives. This is no more than exhorting you to live as Christians and not as Atheists; to live as heirs of immortality not as mere creatures of time; to live not as animals but as children of God. To that result may He sanctify this series of discourses! To that result may He crown them with His blessing!

As I finish this work, I remember that this is the day on which the old Church celebrates with peculiar honor the Resurrection of Jesus. As though it were a new truth, the bells of Easter morning have pealed round the world the glad announcement that he who had slept in the bosom of the earth, at early dawn withdrew the eclipse of death, and broke forth from the sepulchre —the Lord of Life and Glory. And as the mighty declaration echoes in our ears, and our torpid worldliness is shaken, by the rush of angel's feet, is it not *indeed* like a new truth to realize by this Resurrection, that we too shall live forever? That the shadows which fled from the Savior's tomb were as the vails of our own mortality vanishing in the light of God?

If this be so, then let us live no more in shadows but in realities. Let the Prayer that Christ taught us, and which we so often need among the broken passages of life, foretoken the verities and lift us to the communion of heaven!

www.ingramcontent.com/pod-product-compliance
Lightning Source LLC
LaVergne TN
LVHW011209110826
845150LV00006B/1374

* 9 7 8 1 4 2 5 5 1 7 8 1 6 *